WHEN
WORK & FAMILY
COLLIDE

ANDY STANLEY

Keeping Your Job from Cheating Your Family

WHEN WORK & FAMILY COLLIDE

MULTNOMAH
BOOKS

WHEN WORK AND FAMILY COLLIDE

All Scripture quotations, unless otherwise indicated, are taken from the Holy Bible, New International Version®, NIV®. Copyright © 1973, 1978, 1984, 2011 by Biblica Inc.™ Used by permission of Zondervan. All rights reserved worldwide. www.zondervan.com. Scripture quotations marked (NASB) are taken from the New American Standard Bible®. © Copyright The Lockman Foundation 1960, 1962, 1963, 1968, 1971, 1972, 1973, 1975, 1977, 1995. Used by permission. (www.Lockman.org).

Trade Paperback ISBN 978-1-60142-379-5
eBook ISBN 978-1-60142-396-2

Published in the United States by Multnomah, an imprint of the Crown Publishing Group, a division of Penguin Random House LLC, New York.

MULTNOMAH® and its mountain colophon are registered trademarks of Penguin Random House LLC.

Previously published as *Choosing to Cheat*.

The Library of Congress Cataloging-in-Publication data is on file with the Library of Congress.

Printed in the United States of America
2019

10

SPECIAL SALES
Most Multnomah books are available at special quantity discounts when purchased in bulk by corporations, organizations, and special-interest groups. Custom imprinting or excerpting can also be done to fit special needs. For information, please e-mail specialmarketscms@penguinrandomhouse.com or call 1-800-603-7051.

For Bob Walker,

Father of my wife
Grandfather of my children
Example to me

CONTENTS

Who Wins?

Several years ago my wife, Margaret, and I were having dinner with Andy Stanley and his wife, Sandra, as he shared with us his vision for our church. It was a pivotal moment for the leaders and congregation of North Point Community Church, because we had once again outgrown our space. Andy was already preaching twice on Sundays, and it had been suggested that the church start a Saturday night service. As he shared with us that night his hesitation about cutting into his family time on Saturdays, I once again saw the heart and wisdom of this godly man.

Week after week, using the Bible as his guide, Andy teaches and confronts his congregation with the important challenges we all face. One of those challenges is finding a balance between work and family responsibilities. And in this book he eloquently addresses the issue. He asks us: Is there a more important subject than this? Andy believes that for leaders, professionals in all industries, pastors, teachers, homemakers, and parents, the issue is the same—we have a critical need to bring balance to our lives.

Andy asks the tough questions and then gives us some answers about how we can go about accomplishing what may be life's greatest challenge—achieving our goals outside the home when faced with the crucial task of partnering and parenting at home. How can we be successful without sacrificing our relationships with those closest to us?

Andy's answers are biblical, practical, and extremely relevant to our modern way of life. He doesn't pull any punches. He confronts us with truth and transparency. Just as he has made a commitment in his own life to balance his family time with his work, he encourages us to make similar commitments.

This is a life-changing book. And one of the main reasons it's life-changing is that a godly man who makes choices in his own life to never sacrifice his family for success has written it. If he wins the world but loses his family, what has he gained?

Every couple, every parent, and every leader needs to read this book and consider the question: Who wins when my family and work collide?

—Dr. John C. Maxwell

Founder, The John Maxwell Company

Best-selling author of *The 21 Irrefutable Laws of Leadership*

Everybody Cheats

For almost everyone, the word *cheating* has negative connotations, especially if you've ever been cheated. Students cheat in school. Adults cheat on their income taxes. Husbands cheat on their wives. Most of us have cheated in a card game or two.

But allow me to use this unpleasant word in a broader sense. Try thinking of it as simply *choosing to give up one thing in hope of gaining something else of greater value.*

By that definition there's no doubt we're all cheaters. Daily we decide to shortchange one thing in order to more fully experience another. It's especially true with our schedules. We face a variety of responsibilities and opportunities—work, family, hobbies, clubs, sports. The list is endless. Each competes for our attention. Each competes for our most valuable resource: our time. But to give each the time it demands or deserves would require more time than any of us have.

So we "cheat." We give up certain opportunities for the sake of others. We invest in some relationships while neglecting others. We allocate our time the best we can, knowing all the while that somebody's going to feel cheated. Unfortunately, that "somebody" is usually someone we care a great deal about.

Which brings me to the point of this little book.

I've spent hundreds of hours with men and women who've cheated their families for the sake of their career goals. They all admitted knowing there was a problem. They all tried in their own way to dissipate the tension. But they felt trapped. Over time they dreaded coming home. The reception was cold. The conversation was filled with sarcasm used to hide the pain. The discomforts of home drove many to work even longer hours. Others went to the gym. Some to the bar. A few found comfort in the arms of co-workers or friends.

Eventually things unraveled to the point that they had no choice but to seek help. For most there was an event, a wake-up call: *Suddenly* their kids had withdrawn. *Overnight* someone's grades had dropped off. *Out of nowhere* she was more interested in tennis than the family. *Without explanation* intimacy evaporated. But in each case, these were symptoms of something that had been brewing for quite some time.

We all wrestle with the tension between work and family. Regardless of which side of the equation you're on, you know what it's like to deal with the endless cycle of guilt, anger, jealousy, and rejection. Left unattended, these seething emotions have the potential to erode the foundations of even the strongest marriages.

But there's a solution. Strangely enough, the solution is similar to the problem. Both involve "cheating," in that broad sense of giving up one thing to gain something else. Simply put, you must choose to cheat at work rather than at home.

In chapter 1 you'll be introduced to some friends of mine whose struggles typify the experiences of many. In chapters 2 through 5, we'll focus on the dynamic created in the heart of a spouse or child who feels cheated.

Then in part 2 we'll develop a strategy for change. The principles in these final five chapters are drawn largely from the life of a young man who found himself with a dilemma similar to ours. The primary difference being that his *life*, not merely his livelihood, was on the line.

When Work and Family Collide is about establishing priorities. A priority is something you put ahead of something else. A priority is something you say *yes* to even when it means saying no to other important things. Everybody "cheats" like this. It's a principle already at work in your life...one way or another. When you put it to work *for* you, it has the power to transform every facet of your life. When you choose to do so in accordance with God's priorities for your life, it's an invitation for him to bless you in ways you never dared to imagine.

PART ONE

INSIDE THE CHEATED HEART

ONE

When Your World Needs Reordering

Joel Manby entered the work force with all the subtlety of a meteor entering the earth's atmosphere. With an MBA from Harvard and tremendous leadership instincts, he was destined, it seemed, to move from one accomplishment to the next.

Growing up, Joel had watched his father work sunup to sundown plowing fields, mowing lawns, and working in a factory. But somehow the family never seemed to get ahead. With the opportunities Joel had been given to make a better life, he felt a responsibility before God to be a good steward of those prospects. In essence, he felt called by God to achieve his maximum career potential as a servant-leader in business.

And achieve he did.

Upon graduating from Harvard, Joel was offered his dream job—he was one of the first four people hired for a new General Motors start-up soon to be known as Saturn. As part of this groundbreaking team, Joel distinguished himself in the auto industry.

Fueled by that early success, Joel moved up quickly through the GM ranks. His skills, gifts, and work ethic made him perfectly suited for high-level executive leadership. He was destined for the top. At the age of thirty-four, he received an incredible offer to become the president of Saab Cars USA. So he left GM to take on a whole new level of demands. Joel excelled in his new position, and with the success came more responsibility. Joel was soon put in charge of Saab in Asia, South America, and Canada as well. There seemed to be no limit to his future, but at the same time, there seemed to be no end to his frustration.

You see, career wasn't the only arena in which Joel had goals for his life. He and his wife, Marki, had dreams for their family as well. By the time Joel reached his peak at Saab, they had three daughters. While each of Joel's promotions took them a step closer to reaching their financial goals, each demanded more of his time as well. Time that he knew belonged to Marki and the kids.

Marki embraced her role with the same tenacity Joel exhibited in the marketplace. She was committed to being a team player. She didn't always like the hand she was dealt, but she accepted it and did the best she could. She held down the home front while Joel worked to build a bright future for the family. But there was always the frustration, the loneliness, and at times, the anger.

As Joel describes it, "I was traveling more than 50 percent of the time. There were car shows and dealer meetings all the time. And when I was home, I wasn't really there—I had a late-night conference call with Japan or an early-morning conference call with Sweden. In my heart I wanted to be with my family. But I felt like this job was something I had to do. Our family had financial goals, and I felt like God had given me this talent that I should be using. And I viewed each promotion as his reward for a job well done. The truth is, I just couldn't say no. Looking back, it wasn't God prying me away from my family. It was me."

One day, a close friend called Marki to wish her happy birthday. During their casual conversation, a wave of emotions began to surface, surprising even Marki. It was the second year in a row that Joel had been out of town on her birthday. He hadn't forgotten. He just had a job to do. And she had willingly agreed he should go. But somehow, in that moment, Marki was hit with the reality that the very things they were working so hard to achieve were slipping through their fingers with each passing day.

In yet another long-distance phone call, Marki confronted Joel with the painful truth that he was not being the husband or father she had signed up for. In the weeks that followed, Joel and Marki had many heart-to-heart conversations. As Joel began to notice the despair in her countenance, he knew he had to make some major changes. Fast.

"I looked at Marki, and she was bawling her eyes out," he explains. "I knew that if I continued down this path, I was going to lose my family."

Joel made a decision right then and there. He didn't have a plan. He wasn't sure how he could pull off the changes necessary to bring balance to his personal life. He didn't know how he could disentangle himself from his involvement in the car industry. But one thing was certain: He refused to keep going in the direction he was going. Things had to get better. Little did he realize just how bad things would get.

In an attempt to regain control of his life and family, Joel left the international demands of the auto industry for the fast-growing dot-com world. On the morning of April 4, 2000, Joel began his first day as the CEO of a well-funded Internet start-up company, with high hopes for the future. By the end of business on April 4, 2000, it was a very different picture. That day's market plummet marked the beginning of the stock market crash of 2000–2002, which caused the loss of five trillion dollars in the market value of companies, as well as the loss of Joel's hopes for an easy answer to the challenges between work and home. In fact, two weeks into the new company, Joel found himself laying off two-thirds of the company's three hundred employees. The emotional toll of firing two hundred people, combined with twenty-hour workdays, led to more sleepless nights. His first attempt to reclaim the life he wanted led to further distance from Marki and greater desperation.

The remarkable events that followed have had an incredible impact on Joel's life. As he and Marki describe it, the aftermath of Joel's decision to reorder his world was the clearest indication they'd ever experienced of God's presence in their lives and marriage.

FORCED INTO IT

In the midst of their crisis, Joel and Marki heard me share a simple principle that serves as the thesis of this book. On the occasion Joel and Marki heard me share this truth, it was the first time I'd ever said it publicly. I'd been sharing this principle with couples for more than a decade in the privacy of a counseling environment. But for some reason, I never considered the value of sharing this principle in a group setting. Since that time

I've had the opportunity to explain this principle to thousands of business and church leaders, and the response has been overwhelming.

Perhaps the reason I was initially reluctant to talk about this in public is that it highlights a tension I live with every day. This isn't a lesson I've learned and put behind me. This is a principle I have to make a conscious decision to apply daily, or it will slip away. Like many people I know, I love what I do. I rarely have a bad day at the office. My work environment couldn't be any better suited for my gifts and personality. I love to go to work. And like you, I have more to do than I can ever hope to get done. Every afternoon when I leave the office, there are loose ends: phone calls I didn't return, meetings I cut short, and people I didn't get to spend time with who need and deserve my undivided attention.

At the same time, I love my wife and kids. I love to go home. And like you, there's more to do at home than will ever get done. Never once have my kids looked at me and said, "Hey, Dad, we've played enough. Why don't you run back in the house and see if you can get some work done?" Never once has Sandra complained about me coming home too early or doing too many things to help her around the house.

What it boils down to is this: Someone's going to get cheated. Worse yet, somebody's going to *feel* cheated. I'm not giving him or her what is deserved or needed.

In that sense, the issue is never "Am I cheating?" The issue is always "*Where* am I cheating?"

TAKING THE PRESSURE OFF

Everybody holds back, stops short, cuts corners, sets boundaries. You have to. You have several important calls on your life. You have career potential to fulfill, a spouse to love, a family to raise, a ministry to perform. The list goes on. Each of these things has tremendous merit in your life and for the world at large. None of them should be neglected.

However, when you consider the limited number of hours in a day, there's no way you can reach your full potential in all those areas. There's just not enough time.

Your situation isn't that different from mine. If you stayed at work until everything was finished…if you took advantage of every opportunity that came your way…if you sought out every angle to maximize your abilities, improve your skills, and advance your career…you would never go home.

Likewise, if you stayed at home until every ounce of affection was poured out in all the appropriate places…if you kept giving until every emotional need was met…if you did every chore, finished the "honey do" list, and did everything necessary to ensure that everyone felt loved…you would never make it to work.

In fact, if you're a parent, you know that your kids alone could command every waking hour if you let them. Add to that your fitness goals, hobbies, and friendships. The list is endless, and so are the time requirements.

So let me take some pressure off. Your problem is not discipline. Your problem is not organization. Your problem is not that you have yet to stumble onto the perfect schedule. And your problem is not that the folks at home demand too much of your time. The problem is this: there's not enough time to get everything done that you're convinced—or others have convinced you—needs to get done.

As a result, someone or something isn't going to get what he wants from you...what she needs from you...what he deserves from you...certainly not what she *expects* from you. There's no way around it. There's just not enough time in your day to be all things to all people. You're going to have to hold back somewhere. Our knee-jerk reaction to this dilemma is to answer the call of the squeakiest wheel. Whoever creates the biggest mess ends up with the lion's share of our time and attention. We run from fire to fire, troubleshooting our way through life, rescuing the needy and rewarding those who can't seem to stay out of trouble.

But that certainly isn't strategic, and it doesn't solve anything. Over time, our families learn that the only way to get our attention is to create a crisis. And let's face it; it's amazing how much time we can steal from work when our kids are in crisis. Men and women become incredibly bold with their managers, company presidents, and boards when there's a crisis at home. What was unthinkable becomes nonnegotiable.

I know a CEO who spent twenty-nine days with his wife at a detox center six hundred miles from their home. Twenty-nine days. Yet in the previous three years, he had done almost nothing in terms of investing in what he would tell you now is his most important relationship. And if anyone had suggested he take a twenty-nine-day vacation in order to invest in his marriage, he would have laughed. But he did—only when he had to.

I know a contractor who almost had to shut down his business to attend to his daughter's drug addiction. He escorted her from one rehab center to another, trying to find her "the best medical treatment in the country." This is the same guy who could never find the time to complete an entire week of vacation with his family. They left on Saturday; he joined them on Wednesday. But suddenly he has the time.

Wouldn't you do the same for your wife, your husband, and your kids? Of course you would.

So why wait? Instead of allowing the most recent crisis to force the issue, why not be governed by the greatest purpose? Why not "cheat" by design?

But how? How do we scale back at work without destroying our careers? And if you cheat your career goals, won't that end up cheating your family in the long run? Can a home-maker cheat her "to do" list without cheating her family?

These are complex issues. On paper there seems to be no solution. But all is not as it appears. For as we'll see, when we're willing to reprioritize in a way that honors our heavenly Father, he's willing to touch down in the midst of our personal chaos and bring the order and balance we so desperately desire.

A MATTER OF PRINCIPLE

Before we go any further, I need to provide you with a word of warning. As I mentioned earlier, this approach to addressing the collision between work and family is held together by a principle.

Principles are powerful things. In the same way gravity affects everything around the earth, a principle influences everything in your personal universe. Whether you're aware of a principle or not, it still applies. You can ignore it, or you can leverage it. But either way, it goes right on affecting your world. You can break a rule, but not a principle. In fact, by failing to observe a principle, you can break yourself against it.

The principle in this book will cut right to the heart of your priorities. It will test your loyalty and expose your commitment. When exposed to the light of this simple truth, gray areas will suddenly become either black or white. It will reveal your heart as it relates to your family, your work, and your children. This principle will expose your attitude toward your heavenly Father as well. It may upset you. It may offend you. But one thing it won't do is lie. If you're ready to take an honest look at yourself, the choices you've been making and why you make them, you're a candidate for change. My prayer is that you can put this principle to work *for* you, before the consequences of ignoring it have a chance to work *against* you.

TWO

Collision Course

The collision between work and family is inevitable. And is it any wonder? In our culture work and family make up the two most significant arenas of an individual's life. On average a person will spend about one-third of his waking life at work. And for many people, a vast majority of the other two-thirds is dedicated to some part of pursuing or maintaining a family. No other aspects of life are more emphasized in our world than work and family.

Even when you're not working or spending time with family, the influence of those two factors follows you wherever you go. Success or failure in either category will have a direct impact on your overall quality of life, your mental outlook, and your self-esteem.

Your sense of identity is determined largely by work and family. Sociologists, psychologists, and philosophers have conducted thousands of studies on the subject. They've identified hundreds of different factors, from genetic to environmental. But when you categorize all the data, there are basically two things that shape your sense of identity more than anything else: your work and your family.

That's why one of the first questions asked when two people are getting acquainted is, "So, what do you do?" And not far behind are questions such as: "Are you married?" "Do you have any children?" "Do you have any brothers and sisters?"

Knowing *who* you are fulfills a basic human need. Without an answer to that question, a person feels incomplete, inadequate, and insecure. And since work and family play such significant roles in answering it, the pressure is on in both arenas. The natural drive to become established in your career is rivaled only by the desire to have a successful family life. It's only natural that the two become entangled during the rush of daily life.

Yet both work and family originate with the same Source: God. He created them to peacefully coexist. The tension between the two is understandable, but not unavoidable. Whenever there's destructive tension between two things that are designed to work together, it usually points to "operator error."

And when a problem persists, the best thing to do is check with the Manufacturer.

THE ROLE OF WORK

At the climax of creation, God expressed his creativity in an unexpected way:

> The LORD God took the man and put him in
> the Garden of Eden to work it and take care of it.
> (Genesis 2:15)

Before sin, before the fall of man, before the curse, there was work. God made man and placed him in the garden *to work*. From the very beginning, he intended for man to work. Before there was even a family to support, God put Adam to work. It was part of his original plan.

Is that a little surprising? We tend to think of work as being a curse, a consequence of sin. Sure, the nature of work changed a bit after Adam and Eve sinned. God declared that it would be a struggle from then on. He established a relationship between our effort and our provision—a relationship that lures many people to overwork today. Despite those curses, God had the basic concept of work in mind all along. He likes it when we work. He always has. When our attitudes and actions are right, our work is actually very pleasing to God. That's the role of work in its purest form.

Work has been a big part of daily life ever since. Every day, men and women get up at the crack of dawn to plow their vocational fields in order to produce a crop. Presidents lead companies. Salespeople work leads. Homemakers manage households. Some love what they do, and others dream of something better. Whether reluctantly or zealously, we get up each day and work.

THE ROLE OF FAMILY

Whereas work is task focused, the family is relationship focused. One is about doing, while the other is about loving. In one environment we find our worth through accomplishment. In the other we find our value simply by who our relatives are. Work is about doing. Family is about being. The members of my congregation want me to show up prepared to speak. My family is happy if I just show up.

By now you're thinking, "Yeah, yeah, I know all of that. I don't need more insight. I need answers. Give me something practical to do."

That's the task-oriented side of you, the "fix it" thing that goes off inside your head whenever there's a problem. And that's not bad. In fact, it's that side of your personality that makes you so effective on the job. But take that God-given drive for progress and accomplishment home with you, and things start to fall apart. You can't "fix" your family. You can't "fix" your marriage. You can't "fix" your kids.

Family requires an entirely different set of tools and standards of evaluation. You do your job. You love your family. It's when we reverse the order that the tension escalates and the tug of war begins.

BALANCING AGENDAS

In God's original plan there was no conflict between work and family. But when sin entered the world, conflict was introduced into both environments. Man would henceforth struggle at work (see Genesis 3:17–19) and women would feel the pain of childbirth (see Genesis 3:16). And men and women would struggle in their relationships with one another. (See Genesis 3:16, which implies that Eve would have a desire to rule Adam, but in fact, he would rule over her.) The inherent conflict *within each realm* sets us all up to experience conflict *between* these two realms as well.

Creating a healthy family environment is difficult because of the inherent selfishness of each family member. Creating a successful career is difficult because of the competition in the marketplace. Either one of these environments or the struggles related to both could consume our undivided attention. But we don't have the luxury of devoting our undivided attention to either, since most of us find ourselves with the responsibility of both. So we're forced to wrestle with the conflicts of home and work, and the added conflict that arises between the two.

A Strange Twist

With conflict abounding in each of our primary environments, it would seem that our hearts would draw us toward home. After all, despite the relational complexities of family, that's where we're most likely to find unconditional acceptance. In contrast to the turnover in the marketplace, at home we're indispensable. At home we have unique roles. It's within the context of family that we're most likely to have our deepest needs met at the deepest level. Besides, isn't work just a way to provide for the family? Clearly one serves the other.

Strange, isn't it, how on paper it looks so simple, so cause-and-effect? But in reality work becomes far more than a simple means to an end. For many it becomes *the* end. In spite of the challenges that come with any work environment, there's something about it that's captivating. In spite of the futility, in spite of the insecurity, we're drawn to work. The rewards are tangible, progress is measurable, and the accolades are notable. Before long we aren't working to support our families. We're working to support something far less virtuous—our egos.

Now if you're a stay-at-home mom or dad already scheming about how to slip this book into your spouse's briefcase, stop and think. It could be that you struggle with this as well. Maybe you left the job market years ago and you're still uncomfortable telling people that you don't work outside the home. Why is that? Why aren't you content with what you know is the most important job in the world?

Or maybe you struggle with this dynamic in a completely different way. You're fine being a stay-at-home parent. But over time your focus has shifted from the relationship side of staying at home to the task side. You measure your success in terms of neatness, cleanliness, organization, and efficiency. The tasks associated with being a stay-at-home parent are stealing from the joy of being who your partner and children want you to be.

I know of this struggle firsthand as a result of living with the world's most organized woman. Sandra thrives on organization and cleanliness. And I love it. She's incredible when it comes to creating an inviting home environment. But by her own admission, she can become consumed with the environment to the neglect of those who inhabit it.

Just like my marketplace environment, her home environment is full of loose ends. There's always something that needs to be rearranged, organized, cleaned, fixed, replaced, put away, swapped, or returned. Her job is never finished. And to complicate matters, there are four other humans in the house who continually create more for her to do.

The point is, work—whether in or out of the house—can become not only an occupation but also a preoccupation. When that happens, the task steals a piece of us that belongs somewhere else. Before long our families begin to sense it. The people who deserve your undivided attention aren't attended to while the projects that could wait are.

I know this is frustrating. You wish I were there so you could tell me to my face, "You don't understand my situation. It's not as simple as you make it sound." And you're right. I don't know the particulars of your situation. But here's what I do know: Your Creator doesn't define your life by your career achievements or the neatness of your pantry. And neither does he define life by the number of hours you spend with your family. There's no lasting contentment in any of those things. A temporary sense of satisfaction and accomplishment, yes. Contentment, no.

Contentment is found neither in the marketplace nor the family alone. It's found when we align our priorities with his as it relates to both areas of responsibility. There's nothing honoring to God about the workaholic who neglects his or her family. But the man or woman who refuses to provide for the family brings no honor to him either.

Clearly we don't have the luxury of choosing one or the

other, since both are a permanent part of our lives. Both demand more attention than we have to give. Both originated with our Creator. There's not enough time to get it all done. We're going to say no somewhere, either verbally or through neglect. In fact, you're saying no now, whether you realize it or not. And that brings us to the question we'll keep coming back to again and again, a question that, if answered correctly, sets us up to experience the contentment and blessing of God:

Who are you cheating?

Better yet…*Who feels cheated?*

And let me be clear: The place doesn't determine the problem. Stay-at-home moms and dads can just as easily cheat those around them. Whether working outside the home or inside the home, there's a strong tendency to become preoccupied with tasks—agendas and projects and "to do" lists. In either place, you'll be tempted to make work a priority and neglect your most important relationships. Because of our proclivity to focus our attentions on things that stroke our egos (checking off work tasks often does that), it's all too easy for us to cheat those who matter most.

PLAYING THE GAME

When confronted with our misappropriation of time and affection, we're all quick to assure our accusers that we do, in fact, love our families. We talk about what we wish we could do, what we've intended to do, and what we plan to do in the future. We credit ourselves with good intentions. Our guilt is like a salve to our souls. We know we're guilty, but since we know we're guilty, surely there's value in us—surely the fact that we feel bad about what we're doing counts for something! As one young husband blurted out to his wife in his own defense, "But, honey, you know my heart!" And he was right; she knew his heart. But it wasn't his heart that had left her feeling alienated from his life; it was his schedule.

Good intentions have never accomplished anything. If I run over you with my car, but it was my intention to swerve and miss you, you still have to go to the hospital. Upon hearing of my good intentions, your bones are not suddenly healed. You're just as injured as before.

In the physical world, that's all too clear. In the world of relationships, we live with the illusion that good intentions—the desires of our hearts—somehow heal the wounds we've created with our absences and misprioritization. But all we have to do is think back on our own experiences as children to know that nothing could be further from the truth.

If you're a religious person, you may have even taken the "good intention alibi" into the spiritual realm. I've talked to dozens of men and women who have struck a deal with God. This unspoken arrangement goes something like this:

*Lord, you know my heart. You know how badly I want
to spend more time with my family. So while I'm away,
please watch over and protect them. Please fill the void that
I have left while I'm away. Lord, I know you understand
my love for them; help them to understand it as well.*

Granted, you may have never actually prayed a prayer like
that one. But if you are expecting God to do your job for you
while you do a job for somebody else, essentially that prayer
reflects the arrangement you have with God. Now bear with
me while I draw a couple of uncomfortable conclusions from
that approach to dealing with the fact that there isn't enough
time to get everything done. First, we are assuming that God
could not just as easily fill the void at work as he could the void
at home. Second, we are asking God to fill a gap that only we
can fill while we scurry off to do a job that a thousand other
people could do. We might as well pray:

*Dear God, you do what only I can do while I go do what
many others could do just as well or better.*

Kind of convicting, huh?

Does God answer that kind of prayer? I don't know. But in
all my years of counseling, I can tell you something I've never
heard. I've never talked to an adult who reported that while he

was growing up his father worked all the time, but God filled in the gaps, and there was no residual relational or emotional damage. I've never talked to a mom who reported that her husband neglected his family for the sake of his career, but fortunately, God filled the void, and everything was fine.

So where does that leave us? If we can't expect God to cover for us in a way that protects our families from the residual effects of our misprioritization, then what are we to do?

The answer is simple. But it's simple in the way that telling a smoker the solution to his addiction is to stop smoking. It's simple; it's true. But it isn't easy to do.

THREE

Falling Rocks

I met Phyllis Wilson at a leadership conference where she was the keynote speaker. I'd never heard her in person, but I'd certainly heard of her. In a relatively short time, Phyllis had established herself as somewhat of an expert in the field of adolescent behavior and family systems. Her education and her platform ability were a winning combination.

Within the first few minutes of her talk, I knew why Phyllis had become such a sought-after conference speaker. She was one of the most gifted communicators I'd ever heard. Frankly, I was somewhat intimidated by her ability to connect so quickly with the audience. Afterward we had an opportunity to chat, and to my surprise she asked if she could come by and talk to me at my office. The tone of her question suggested that she had something specific on her mind. The stage persona quickly drained from her face and was replaced by what I read as panic.

One week later Phyllis showed up in my office looking like she'd just come down with the flu. Her face was pale, and it appeared that she was having trouble breathing. She barely muttered hello as she slumped down in the chair across the desk from me. "Are you okay?" I asked.

Phyllis wasn't sick, at least not physically. On the night before I heard her speak, she'd come home from another speaking engagement and found a note from her husband, Jimmy, on the pillow. The gist of the note was that he wanted out.

As you might imagine, I began asking questions: Was there another woman? Had there been a big fight? Were there financial issues? Was substance abuse a part of their lives? Was there a problem with the kids?

To these questions Phyllis shook her head. She said, "I'm completely at a loss. He leaves me messages insisting that I pack up and go, but he won't talk to me. He says there's nothing to talk about."

As I read Jimmy's note, there was no bitterness or anger in his tone. There was no reason given. It was as if he assumed they both understood what the issue was and that no further discussion was necessary.

Phyllis stared out the window, trying to come up with something to explain Jimmy's behavior. Then she turned back in my direction and shrugged. So I asked her again about the recent past: Was there an event? a defining moment? What did their most recent argument center on?

The last question sparked some interest.

"Argue? That's just it. We never argue," she said.

"About anything?" I asked.

"No," she replied, "in fact we've prided ourselves in the fact that unlike most couples, we don't have arguments."

Now I was starting to understand. So I asked, "If Jimmy were sitting here and I asked him what one thing he would like to change in your marriage, what do you think it would be?"

She managed a smile and said, "Before all of this I would have said he wanted me to be home more. But now I don't know. Now he doesn't want me there at all."

Phyllis finally broke down and began to cry. I say finally, because up until this time, she'd done a pretty good job retaining her composure. But when she broke, the tears flowed.

Eventually I made contact with Jimmy, and he agreed to come in and talk. But he assured me that he wasn't going to change his mind and that it would be a waste of my time to try and convince him to do so. I assured him that I was just trying to help Phyllis understand what was going on and that I didn't think it was my responsibility to change anybody's mind.

As it turned out, Phyllis was right. There was no landmark incident that culminated in Jimmy's request. There was no other woman. And she was right about there not being a big argument. Jimmy nodded in agreement when Phyllis reiterated her claim that they never argued.

So what was going on? Why this abrupt shift in affection? Why was Phyllis clueless as to why Jimmy suddenly wanted her out?

THE ARRANGEMENT

Jimmy and Phyllis had an arrangement, not unlike most couples. When Phyllis's career as a conference speaker began to blossom, Jimmy felt like it was his responsibility to be her biggest supporter. As a website developer, Jimmy had the option of working out of his home and chose to do so in order to give Phyllis the flexibility she needed to travel and leverage her opportunities.

Way to go, Jimmy! What a guy. Probably ought to be nominated as husband of the year. That's what Phyllis thought, and she was quick to give him the credit he deserved. While she was away, he held down a full-time job and took care of their two kids.

Now all of that looked good on paper. And everybody's heart was in the right place.

But over time something began to happen in the Wilson household. Nobody could see it, but everybody could feel it. And when they felt it, they wrote it off to "That's what we agreed to do."

"Mommy's not here tonight. But she's helping other mommies and daddies know how to be better mommies and daddies for their children."

"I'll be gone again next week, but this engagement has the potential to open an entirely new set of doors for us. I'll sure miss you."

"We'll be fine. We'll miss you, but we'll be okay. What you're doing is important."

Phyllis was cheating at home. And Jimmy wasn't saying anything about it. Phyllis was taking what belonged at home and selling it to strangers at conferences, and Jimmy was cheering her on. And everybody—with the exception of the kids—was smiling on the outside but dying on the inside. Nobody wanted to admit it, but the arrangement wasn't working, at least not in the way it was being played out.

Jimmy didn't want to nag. After all, this was what he agreed to. Phyllis was starting to believe her own press, and she liked what she was hearing. Add to that, her income was almost double what Jimmy was bringing home. And as much as she loved her family, life on the road was...well...like a continuous party.

Consequently, it was easy for Phyllis to ignore the internal red flags that periodically waved right in front of her face. And when she backed out of the driveway with that perennial cloud of guilt hanging over her, she would remind herself, "This is what we agreed to."

As you might imagine, it was more difficult for Jimmy to maintain a smiling face. Life at home with the kids was no continuous party. But after a while he became accustomed to Phyllis's absences. In fact, her arrivals began to feel more like interruptions than homecomings. He confided in me, "I got to the point where I would have been just as happy if she'd simply mailed us a check and gone on to her next engagement."

Sound extreme? It is. But don't make the mistake of taking comfort in the fact that your situation isn't that extreme. For a long time theirs wasn't either. In the beginning their situation was like yours...or possibly better. I say that not to scare you but to wake you up to an insidious dynamic that slowly takes its toll on families who have arrangements like the Wilsons'.

HOLDING ON

Use your imagination for just a moment. Imagine that your best friend walks up to you in your front yard one Saturday and asks you to do him a favor. You have some free time, and so you oblige. He walks over to his car, pops the trunk, and produces a thirty-pound rock.

Now here's where you're really going to have to use your imagination.

At this point he hands you the rock and says, "I really need you to stand here with this rock until I return." He explains why it's important that you stand in that one spot with the rock and that he'll return shortly to retrieve it. It's a strange request, and his explanation doesn't make a lot of sense, but this is someone you trust, so you agree. At this point he thanks you profusely and then hops into his car and drives away.

An hour goes by. And what started out as a feasible favor is beginning to get a little hard. But after all, this is your best friend, so you suck it up and stand there. Another hour goes by, and your arms are starting to ache. Everything in you wants to sit down, but you made a promise. Then suddenly, to your relief, your friend pulls in the driveway, jumps out of the car, and runs in your direction. You're so relieved. If you weren't holding the rock, you would hug him.

But your joy is quickly extinguished. Instead of relieving you of your burden, he says, "Look, I told you I was coming right back. I was delayed. Here's the deal. I need to run one more quick errand. If you'll keep holding the rock, I'll make it up to you when I return." Once again, you trust that what you're told is true. If your friend needs to run one more errand before relieving you, that's just the way it is. So you agree. As he turns to go, you can't help but blurt out, "Please hurry."

Off your friend goes, and there you stand.

Another hour goes by. The sun begins to set. Your muscles are screaming at you to drop the rock. But you refuse to give in. You're committed to holding up your part of the bargain. Besides, your friend said he would make it up to you. You aren't sure what that means, but it must be something good.

Thirty minutes later a car pulls up in the driveway. But someone you don't know is driving. This person walks over and, almost in a whisper, informs you that your friend has been delayed. "Would you mind holding the rock for just a little while longer?" he asks.

The expression on your face is a mixture of pain and anger. You manage to mutter, "Whatever. Just tell him to hurry."

Away the person goes, and there you stand. It's dark now. The streets are empty. The neighbors are huddling at their windows watching you stand there, wondering why you would put up with being treated like that by a "friend."

Another hour goes by. You begin to lose your grip. Your arms begin to fall. You tell yourself to hold on, but your body just won't respond. Down goes the rock. And just as it hits the pavement and disintegrates into a hundred pieces, your friend pulls up in the driveway. He jumps out of the car, runs over with a look of panic on his face, and asks, "What happened? Did it slip? Did somebody knock it out of your hands? Did you change your mind?" And as he looks for an explanation as to why you *suddenly* dropped the rock, you know that it was a long time coming.

THE EXHAUSTION FACTOR

Now let me explain what happened in terms that will help us later on. Your mental willingness was overcome by your physical exhaustion. You wanted to do what you were asked to do, but after a while you just couldn't do it anymore. Add to that the frustration of being misled about how long you would have to stand there. But even if the aggravation is put aside, at some point you just weren't going to be able to keep holding on. No amount of love, dedication, commitment, or selflessness was going to be able to make up for the fact that your arms were worn out.

Now, just for fun, let's add another element to the story.

You're about to pass out from exhaustion. And finally a car pulls up in the driveway. You're so angry and in so much pain you know you'll have to choose your words carefully. Sure enough, it's your buddy. He walks over slowly with one hand behind his back. He forces a smile and says, "I brought you something."

Suddenly, he whips out from behind his back a bouquet of flowers. At that point you don't merely drop the rock, you muster just enough strength to throw it at him! And as he ducks, he exclaims, "What was that all about? I brought you flowers, didn't I?"

THE SOUND OF FALLING ROCKS

I probably don't need to apply my little parable. The meaning is pretty obvious. So at the risk of insulting your intelligence, let me be painfully specific:

- When we ask our husbands and wives to carry our loads as well as theirs, it's like handing them the rock.
- When we're absent at critical junctures in family life, they're left holding the rock.
- When we find ourselves pointing to the future to somehow make up for the past and the present, they're holding the rock.
- When we assure our families that things are going to change, and they don't, they're holding the rock.

The interesting thing is, they always accept it. And why not? They love us. They trust us. Besides, we always reassure them that they'll only have to hold it for a short time.

Everybody is willing to be understanding when a loved one has to pull back on family time. In real life it's unavoidable from time to time. But when our families are left to carry loads they weren't created to carry, it's just a matter of time before things begin to unravel.

There's a point at which that mental willingness succumbs to something our families have no control over. With a literal rock, mental willingness is eventually overcome by physical exhaustion. With the figurative rock, mental willingness is eventually overcome by emotional exhaustion. And when that happens, the rocks come tumbling down.

There's always a final straw: a comment, a phone call, a tired explanation, a no-show, a forgotten birthday, or a missed game. Some little thing that pushes those we love past their ability to hold on. And to the uninformed, unsuspecting spouse—to the husband or wife who has lived with the fantasy that everything's just fine—it seems like a huge overreaction.

"All I said was…"

"All I did was…"

But it wasn't the moment. It wasn't the phone call. It wasn't the fact that the big hand was on the six instead of the twelve. It was weeks, months, or possibly years of cheating. The rock finally slipped out of their callused hands.

You always know when the rock has dropped. There's never any mistaking it. Your straight-A student is failing. Nobody runs to greet you at the door when you finally arrive. Your husband or wife has lost all interest in being intimate.

You hear things such as: "I just can't do this anymore!" "I can't pretend anymore!" "I've had enough of your promises!" "I feel like a single parent!"

When the rock drops, you'll do everything in your power to pick it up and piece it back together. As we mentioned in the previous chapter, you'll find the time to devote to fixing the problem. But in my experience, when the rock drops, there's always some permanent damage. Most rocks can't be put back together again.

FOUR

Picking Up the Pieces

I'm going to tell you a secret about your family members that they'll never tell you themselves, primarily because they aren't aware of it. But it's true and extremely important for you to know.

This little secret explains why cheating at home has such a devastating effect on the emotions of our family members. Ironically, it also explains why they're so eager to take the rock in the first place.

Do you know what your family wants from you more than anything else?

"Love?" you say.

That's part of it. But it goes deeper than that. They want to feel accepted. In practical terms they want to feel like they're your priority.

"But they *are* my priority," you might argue.

Granted. They may be your priority, but that's not my point. They want to *feel* like your priority. It's not enough for them to *be* your priority. They must *feel* like it.

I'll never forget discussing this point with a very busy corporate vice president. He kept assuring me how much he loved his wife and kids. Finally I interrupted him and said, "The problem is, you love your family in your heart, but you don't love them in your schedule. And they can't see your heart."

Every member of your family is an acceptance magnet. Their hearts are drawn toward acceptance. They want to feel your acceptance, your approval, and yes, your love. If you're having trouble connecting the dots, think back to your own childhood. How important was it for you to feel like a priority in your father's world? If you grew up wondering where you fit in his list of priorities, you know the myriad of confusing emotions that filled your childhood and adolescence.

If you grew up with the security of knowing you and the family were clearly *the* priority of his life, you'll have a difficult time imagining what it would feel like to grow up without that. But as an adult you can understand the important role his visible love played in your development.

The same is true of your relationship with your mom. Imagine growing up in a home where you had to compete for your mother's attention and affection. Perhaps you don't have to imagine; perhaps you remember. Either way, looking back it's easy for us to understand and appreciate the importance of a family environment where moms, dads, and kids feel like they're the priority.

A measure of loyalty is assumed in every relationship. The more intimate the relationship, the greater the expectation. Think about your wedding vows…okay, so you can't remember. Well, I bet you said something indicating that your spouse was going to be your priority over everything and everybody else. Remember that? It was perfectly appropriate to make that kind of commitment. And now it's perfectly appropriate for your spouse to expect that kind of commitment.

MAKING THE CONNECTION

Now, here's the point: our families' willingness to hold the rock for us is born out of their desire to please us.

Part of their reason for wanting to please us is that in pleasing us they hope to gain what they value most, our acceptance. They say yes with the hope that their sacrifices will result in a deeper sense of appreciation and love. Their hope is that if they please us, we'll find them even more acceptable. Taking the rock—compensating for our busyness, putting up with our absences—is a way to capture and maintain our affection.

There's almost nothing our families wouldn't agree to do if we asked. To refuse our requests is to run the risk of disappointing us and possibly losing what's most important. So initially they give us a look that communicates "count on me" and they say, "No problem." But over time the enthusiasm wanes. Over time their looks become ones of intense disappointment. And they're barely able to muster a simple, "We understand."

Now don't check out. This isn't psychobabble. This is a dynamic that's at work right now in the hearts of your spouse and children. This is a dynamic that's at work in your heart as well. Let's face it, why do you work so hard? Part of the reason is so that you can *gain approval*. It's not just about the money and the financial security. You want to know you're okay. And somewhere out there in the marketplace, you've found an environment that says you're okay when you perform at a certain standard.

And that's perfectly acceptable. God created you to seek and find approval. That underlying need provides the context for our relationship with him and everyone else we come into contact with. Again, we're acceptance magnets. We're drawn to environments where our egos are stroked. We flee from environments fraught with rejection.

Here's the problem. When we leave our families holding

the rocks for too long, their sacrifice becomes a source of the very thing they dread the most—rejection. They go along with us to find approval, and in time the rocks that looked like means to greater acceptance become symbols of rejection. And the longer they hold them, the more rejected they feel.

Whenever you compromise the interests of a family member in order to fill gaps somewhere else, you shuffle your priorities. Loyalty that was intended for a loved one gets displaced and given to someone else. However small, it increases the emotional load he or she must carry. It may not seem like a big deal. But it sends the message: *You're important…but right now something else is more important.* When we take advantage of a family member's willingness to support our dysfunctional schedules and misprioritization, we send a message of rejection.

When you take loyalty that belongs to your family and give it to someone else—your boss, manager, supervisor, co-workers, potential clients, or investors—family members don't feel as if you aren't being as loyal as you should be. They feel rejected.

Again, that's not what you intend to communicate. But actions speak louder than intentions. Nobody can see your heart. Displaced loyalty is translated into rejection, the very thing your family fears most from you.

From your perspective, you're just trying to survive. You have a dozen good reasons to justify shifting your priorities to meet the ever-changing demands at work. But in the economy of human emotions, that distinction isn't recognized. If something's more urgent, it must be more important. At least that's how it's perceived and interpreted by your loved ones.

THE CLIENT

Let's get specific. When you can't have dinner with your family because you "can't get out of" having dinner with a client who just flew into town, you send a message to your family: "These clients are more important to me than you." I know that's not how you feel. But how *you* feel is irrelevant. Explaining the importance of the dinner meeting may get them to nod their heads in agreement. But the message is still the same: "Tonight, my priority is somebody else."

Are there times when you're going to be out late? Of course. Are there weeks when you'll need to travel? Absolutely. But understand, the message you send is the same. And if you send enough of those messages, they'll eventually chip away at the confidence your spouse and kids cling to—confidence that *they* are your priority.

Our instinct is to share our dilemma, seeking empathy and understanding. We think if we can just explain the urgency of the situation, it will somehow change the way everything's interpreted. But in the end, it always feels the same. Cheating at home is translated as rejection. Everything and everyone else are greater priorities, even people we haven't met.

GAUGING OUR SUCCESS

This whole thing would be much easier if members of our families had gauges on their foreheads. Gauges are the great thing about cars; you know exactly where you stand. If you run out of gas, it's your own fault. If the engine overheats, you saw it coming.

Wouldn't it be great if our spouses and kids had little acceptance meters? We could come home at the end of the day and check everyone's reading. Then we would know who needs a little extra time and attention. We would know when everybody was charged up enough so it would be safe to ask for a night out with clients. Then we would know when it's appropriate to expect intimacy with our spouses and when we should move in another direction. When everybody was down to a quarter of a charge, we could plan a vacation. Wouldn't that just simplify everything?

Men and women generally respond differently when I suggest the beauty of such a system. The men get all teary-eyed thinking about how much simpler life would be. Women, on the other hand, shake their heads in disagreement. And I know what they're thinking. Women don't want a gauge; they want to be figured out. Taking the time to figure a woman out makes her feel valued.

Now I'm not sure why that is. Women watch men read manuals, pore over articles, and spend countless hours tinkering with stuff, and then we simply ask them, "Hey, what's wrong?"

Now, guys, you may hate me for putting this in print for your wife to read, but I don't know any other way to communicate it. You've never walked into your office and asked your computer, "What's wrong?" You've never said to your transmission, "What's wrong?" You've never asked your wide-screen television for a self-diagnosis.

So when you ask your wife to give you a reading, is it any wonder that she says, "Nothing"? Unfortunately for us men, our wives and kids didn't come equipped with gauges. But somewhere between gauges and "nothing," couples must find common ground for the sake of monitoring the vital signs of the family. It's up to each of us to monitor the emotional weight being carried by each of our family members. Through honest, and sometimes awkward, communication we can learn to monitor the hearts of our loved ones.

The gauges on your dashboard aren't there to tip you off to the fact that your car is in need of repair. They're there to keep things from getting to that point. When your car breaks down, you don't need a gauge; it's obvious. The advantage of learning to monitor the hearts of our family members is that it enables us to avoid a crisis rather than figure out how to recover from one.

Sandra is the finest woman I've ever met. She's a wonderful wife to me and a loving mother to our children. There's nothing in the world she wouldn't do for us. I'm convinced she would follow me to the edge of the world if I asked her. She'd even do most of the driving.

Ironically, it's Sandra's intense dedication to the family that makes her hard to read sometimes. Her laid-back manner and endless energy make it easy for me to presume too much. And early on in our marriage, I took unfair advantage of her desire to be supermom. Like every couple, we had to learn to read the gauges.

My children are the same way. If I judged by appearances alone, I'd have no way of knowing when their gauges were in the red. Like most kids, they each crave Dad's attention. So when I show up, they light up. It would be easy to make incorrect assumptions about what's going in their hearts.

So in our house we have a very simple system. First, Sandra and I have agreed to avoid saying, "Nothing" when it is untrue. Instead of asking, "What's wrong?" we say something like, "I can tell something's bothering you. When you want to talk about it, I'm available." When I'm having a hard time reading the gauges and need a little help, I say to Sandra, "How are we doing?" That's my way of saying, "I think we're doing all right around here; what do you think?"

When our kids were small, we were more specific. At least twice a week at bedtime, I would ask each of them this series of questions:

- Is everything okay in your heart?
- Did anyone hurt your feelings today?
- Are you mad at anyone?
- Did anyone break a promise to you?
- Is there anything I can do for you?

That fourth question was really important to me. I've accidentally promised my kids stuff many times. I say "accidentally" because my "I'll think about it" seemed to always sound like a promise to my kids.

FINDING YOUR GROOVE

Now all of that may sound rote. And the last thing you need is another list to remember. But the point is, you've got to slow down long enough to check your family's vital signs. We're all better at this than we would like to admit. We generally know when something's up. I say that based on the testimonies of countless couples who all admitted they knew things weren't right. When the rocks dropped, they weren't completely surprised. We're rarely blindsided by problems on the home front.

The real issue is whether we're willing to pull out of the fast lane long enough to find out what's going on.

Slowing down to read the vital signs isn't easy. But it's a whole lot easier than getting out of the race completely in order to handle a major crisis.

THE DIVISION TITLE

The reality of this dynamic became even clearer to me the first year our boys played recreation league baseball. On the first and third Wednesdays of each month, I have a meeting that lasts well past 10:00 p.m. On those particular Wednesdays, I stay at the office throughout the afternoon and arrive home after the kids are asleep. When our two boys started playing Little League baseball, I sat down with them and explained that I would have to miss some of their Wednesday evening games because of my meeting schedule.

Because each of them played two games a week, I would still be able to attend the majority of their games. They understood (there's that word again). In fact, I had Sandra call me in the middle of my meetings when either of our boys got a hit. I could look down at my phone, see her number, and without having to answer know that things were going well on the baseball field.

At the end of that first season, both of my boys' teams had

a good chance to win their respective divisions. As I looked at the calendar, however, I saw that my oldest son, Andrew, would have his deciding game on a Wednesday evening when I was scheduled to be at the office. Well, there was no way I was going to miss his game, so I told our business administrator I wouldn't be able to attend our meeting. I never mentioned this to Andrew. Actually, I didn't really think he kept up with which Wednesday nights I was out and which ones I was available. But I was mistaken.

The evening before the big game, we were having dinner and I mentioned how much I was looking forward to his game. He immediately looked up at me and said, "But what about your meeting?" I was really surprised. Andrew was only nine at the time, but he was keeping up. I smiled and told him I'd canceled my meeting so that I could be at his game. His eyes lit up. He'd been under the impression that I wasn't coming. The look on his face told me that I'd just made a major deposit with my oldest son. It was one thing for me to be there; it was something else entirely for me to cancel something in order to attend.

They won their game that Wednesday night. Two nights later they beat the best team in the league. Andrew hit a triple and drove in the go-ahead run. His team went on to win the division championship, and he added another trophy to his collection.

Everyone's busy. All of us have more to do than we'll ever

get done. We all have to prioritize some things and slight others. When you do this strategically, you leverage your busyness for the sake of what's most important. Then you communicate the message our families long to *feel:* "You are important to me. You're more important to me than anybody or anything else in my world."

FIVE

Double-Edged Sword

Once again, if you are dying to figure out a way to get your workaholic husband or wife to examine his or her schedule through the lens of these truths, I would suggest you pause long enough to first examine the log in your own eye. My experience is that men and women who cheat at home get way too much support from the people they're cheating.

Remember Phyllis and Jimmy from chapter 3? When I had a chance to meet with Jimmy, he insisted that their family problems stemmed solely from Phyllis's unwillingness to properly govern her speaking schedule. In his words, "She abandoned the family for life on the road."

After about five minutes of listening to him whine, I held up my hand (terrible counseling technique, I admit) and asked him a question. I said, "Jimmy, did you ever suggest packing up the kids and going with her?"

"Of course not," he said. "The kids are in school, and I have a job to do."

"So," I said, "there's something more important to you than keeping the family together."

He looked puzzled.

I continued. "My point is, you're certain that your family problems stem from Phyllis's unwillingness to prioritize correctly, but aren't you guilty of the same thing?"

He continued to look puzzled.

I pressed on. "What did you do to get Phyllis off the road?"

"Well, we talked about it from time to time," Jimmy said.

"And how did those conversations resolve?" I asked.

"She would agree and promise to cut back," he said, "but nothing changed."

"And what did you do?"

He shrugged and said, "Nothing. What could I do?"

"So you're really a victim, aren't you?" I said.

"Yeah, I guess I am."

Now, I don't do much counseling. The reason being, I'm not good at it. It's not that I lack insight. What I lack is patience, tact, etiquette. So at this point in the conversation, I took off my counselor's hat and put on my judge's robe and told Jimmy what a lousy husband and father I thought he was.

Just kidding.

What I did tell him was that if all he'd done so far was have a few tame conversations with Phyllis about their situation, he was as much to blame for their crisis as she was.

"What else could I do?" he asked.

"Well, if you'd come to me before the most current crisis," I said, "and if she refused to reduce her travel, I would have suggested you pack up and go with her."

"That would have wreaked havoc with our kids and our finances," he said.

Finally, I regained my counseling composure and paused. I waited a long time until what he had just said began to sink in.

He smirked. "I get it."

He leaned back, stared out the window, and said, "The kids are a wreck as it is, and I can't concentrate at work. I don't know if it would have gotten her off the road, but I doubt it would have made matters any worse."

LOVE AND LEARN

Jimmy and I went on to talk about all the ways he contributed to the problem. By the time we were finished, he admitted that he had major reservations about her road trips to begin with.

He wanted to support his wife's budding career. No one can blame him for that. But looking back, the timing was terrible and he knew it but was afraid to put his foot down.

Afraid of what? Afraid of the thing we all fear in family relationships: rejection. As is so often the case, Jimmy took the rock to avoid rejection and, as a result, felt the full force of it. He thought he was being a loving, understanding spouse, when in reality he was simply facilitating his own failure as a husband and father. And one day he just couldn't handle it anymore, and the rock dropped. His emotional exhaustion overwhelmed his willingness to be a supportive husband. What he wanted so badly to avoid became a raging reality. And to compound his confusion, now he looked like the bad guy for tearing the family apart.

Husbands and wives are hesitant to "put a stake in the ground" because they feel like they're betraying their commitment to be supportive spouses. Nothing could be further from the truth. Unfortunately, men and women wait so long that by the time they finally do something, they're so exhausted they feel like their only option is to bail out completely.

To facilitate your husband's or wife's misprioritization is to add to your own dysfunction. Sure it's uncomfortable to take a stand. But it's only going to get more uncomfortable with time. I know it feels like you're being unsupportive. But the truth is, you're supporting what needs supporting most. All of us need a reality check every once in a while. Nobody stays on the right side of the road without lines and guardrails. On more than one occasion, Sandra has looked at me and said, "I'm beginning to feel like a single parent."

Mutual Submission

If you're a Christian, you may find yourself wrestling with issues of submission and unconditional love and a myriad of other biblical concepts that support your paradigm for marriage. Maybe you do remember your marriage vows. Perhaps your takeaway from everything the pastor had you repeat that Saturday afternoon was, "Grin and bear it." How else could you interpret, "Till death do us part"?

But before you hunker down for another season of neglect, you need to know that you're not getting any brownie points in heaven. Submission has nothing to do with fulfilling a role you weren't designed to fill. That's not submission. That's emotional suicide. God isn't going to honor that.

Facilitating your husband's or wife's irresponsible behavior and unhealthy priorities is not an act of love. You wouldn't consider it an act of love for someone to sell your underage son or daughter a pack of cigarettes, would you? Why not? Well, because it's not good for them.

Exactly.

Now I'm sure I'll have to fight with my publisher to keep this next sentence in my manuscript, but I surely believe it with all my heart. If your marriage is headed toward a crisis anyway, go ahead and have it while you still have your wits about you. Call the question. Show up at work. Pack up the kids. Hide the keys. Do something. But for your sake and the sake of your marriage, don't wait until you're so beaten down that there seems to be only one option.

THE SUPREME EXAMPLE

As a Christian, I believe we find in Christ an example of unconditional love and a call to uncompromising accountability. He laid down his life for us. But he told us how to live in no uncertain terms. He saw no contradiction between the two, because there is none.

Christ honored us by considering our needs before his own. At the same time, he honors us by laying down the laws of relationship and holding us accountable to them. He promises to never leave or forsake us in one breath and yet warns us of the practical consequences of refusing to honor the Son in the next. He accepts us the way we are but loves us too much to leave us in our original state. He submitted himself, while at the same time, he requires our submission. It's through mutual submission that the created and the Creator experience intimacy. And so it is with a husband and wife.

WORK IT OUT

So what does that look like in your marriage? Unfortunately, I can't tell you that. But suffering in silence is not an option. Complaining to your friends isn't a solution either.

Whatever you do, don't sit idly by while your self-esteem slowly erodes. Don't allow the current dysfunction to continue chipping away at your ability to cope with the normal stresses of everyday life. Do something now while you're still strong enough to weather the ensuing storm. Do something now before you feel like your only option is to run.

Regardless of how strong or committed you are, eventually you'll exceed your emotional limits. Sooner or later, mental willingness will be overcome by emotional exhaustion. When you reach that point, you'll do something. But odds are it will be something you regret.

That's precisely what happened to Jimmy. Rather than confront Phyllis, he waited. In fact, he waited and prayed. He prayed that God would change Phyllis's heart and bring her home. But God didn't answer his prayer. And so when he couldn't handle it anymore, he did the very thing he criticized her for. He left.

As bad as things were, Jimmy regrets the decision. He regrets it primarily for his children's sake. It's a memory he hopes time will erase. And maybe it will. But in the meantime, Jimmy can't forget the panicked looks on his kids' faces as he gathered their belongings, hurriedly packed their suitcases, and rushed out the door before Phyllis arrived. For him those two days were a nightmare he relives again and again. In the eyes of his children, he saw insecurity he had never seen before.

Was he wrong to leave? I don't know. But I'm glad something happened. For the first time they're talking about a situation that should have been addressed years ago. Phyllis doesn't want to give up her traveling completely, but she sees the value in cutting back.

Although it took awhile, Jimmy is able to see how his good intentions contributed to their issues. He's still angry. But he realizes that part of his anger is self-directed. He's learning to say no to Phyllis. And strangely enough, I think she actually likes it.

HOME SECURITY

In the next section we're going to address in very specific terms what to do when there's too much to do. But before we shift gears, I want to draw your attention one last time to the relationship between cheating at home and the emotional strain it creates. Every time you cheat your family—no matter how trivial—it represents a draw against someone's emotional strength. Every time.

Regardless of how much money you have in the bank, when you make a withdrawal, you have a little less. Regardless of how happy and healthy your family is, when you take what's expected at home and give it to someone or something else, you've made a withdrawal. If the deposits don't vastly outnumber the withdrawals, there'll be tension. The tension will ruin the joy of coming home. When you no longer enjoy coming home, you'll look for more reasons to stay away. That, of course, only makes things worse.

If there were physical rocks or visible gauges, our jobs would be easier. It would be next to impossible for us to lose sight of this important relationship. But there are no rocks. And the family doesn't come equipped with gauges. Yet the relationship is there. It's real. The emotional and relational well-being of our families is at stake. The moral well-being of our children is at stake. And we have the change in our pockets to ensure that the necessary deposits are made on time.

This is difficult work. But it's your only unique responsibility. On the marketplace side of the equation, you're expendable. Even if you own your own company, you're expendable. You know that. At home you play a unique role. You're the only father or mother your children will ever have. The health of your marriage determines the environment in which your kids grow up.

Even if the tension in your family never reaches crisis proportion, why allow any unnecessary tension? Why not address the undercurrents? Your home environment defines what your children perceive as normal. Create for them what you hope they'll re-create when it's their turn.

I know what you're thinking: "But what about my job? What about my career? So far you've done nothing to help me know how to balance all of that."

We'll get to those concerns next. But as we'll see in the beginning of the next section, *what* precedes *how*. Until you've made up your mind to quit cheating at home, it's pointless to talk about how everything's going to pan out. You have to make up your mind before you determine the feasibility of your decision.

Sound backward? This isn't the first time you've approached a decision this way.

Remember when you decided to get married? Did you have all the how-tos worked out? Probably not. You decided marriage was the thing to do, and you went for it. And once the decision was made, you came up with a workable plan. It entailed some sacrifice and some creative financing. But you made it work. Why? Because love conquers all!

You're going to need the same passion and blind determination with this decision as you did with that one. And when you do, you'll have made more than a domestic decision. You'll have made a spiritual one as well. For in choosing to put your family first, you've brought your priorities in line with those of your heavenly Father. And when you surrender your will to the Father, he takes responsibility for the outcome of the journey.

PART TWO

STRATEGY FOR CHANGE

We should not be surprised to find this principle illustrated in Scripture. In fact, this principle is found throughout Scripture. Chances are, your favorite Bible story involves someone giving to God what somebody else believed belonged to him. And the reason you love the story is because God came through on behalf of the individual who "cheated" man rather than God. Daniel was one such man. Actually, at the time of this story, Daniel was only a teenager…

SIX

Tale of Two Kings

About 605 BC the Babylonians invaded Jerusalem. Rather than destroy the nation itself, the Babylonians sought instead to destroy the Israelites' identity and culture. They made Israel a slave state. As part of the process, they hand-picked the best and the brightest of the youth and shipped them off to be immersed in Babylonian culture and turned into model Babylonians. Daniel was among the potential converts. He was taught a new language and given a new wardrobe and a new name.

Apparently, Daniel was okay with these changes. But then

his new masters demanded something of Daniel that he couldn't go along with.

> Then the king ordered Ashpenaz, chief of his court officials, to bring into the king's service some of the Israelites from the royal family and the nobility—young men without any physical defect, handsome, showing aptitude for every kind of learning, well informed, quick to understand, and qualified to serve in the king's palace. He was to teach them the language and literature of the Babylonians. The king assigned them a daily amount of food and wine from the king's table. (Daniel 1:3–5)

Daniel drew the line when it came to his diet. Eating from the king's table had overtones that Daniel wasn't comfortable with. It wasn't so much the food as much as it was what the food symbolized. Traditionally, the Babylonians worshiped their pagan gods through offerings of meat and wine. After they offered the meat and wine to the gods, the leftovers were eaten by the king and his court as a final gesture of loyalty. Eating the food offered to the Babylonian gods was a symbol of submission to their authority. By eating the food, participants acknowledged the gods as the source of their provision and strength. In Daniel's case it would, in effect, be giving the Babylonian gods

72

credit for his wisdom and abilities. And that constituted a clear violation of Daniel's loyalty to the God of Israel.

Humanly speaking, Daniel had every reason to go along with the demands of his captors. Why remain loyal to a God who had so clearly abandoned him? Daniel had been forcefully taken from his home. His family was probably missing or dead. He'd been stripped of his identity. His nation and culture had been destroyed. Why remain loyal to a God who would allow all of that? Besides, this was his big break.

Instead of killing him, they were grooming him to be a model citizen. Instead of being assigned to some meaningless work detail, he was being trained to serve in the king's palace. Instead of starving, he was offered the same food the king ate. Why rock the boat? Besides, what was God going to do? What more could he do? Everything of any value had already been taken away.

Daniel had no reason to fear God. The damage was done. It was time for Daniel to fend for himself. Or at least it would seem so.

Daniel's situation was not unlike ours. There were two parties who wanted something from Daniel, and he couldn't satisfy the demands of both. He would either give the visible king, King Nebuchadnezzar, what he expected or give the invisible King, the Lord God, what he deserved. There was no way to satisfy both. He could either violate his conscience and hope

God would understand or violate the king's expectations and hope the Babylonians would understand.

Now think about it. Which would you have chosen? In one corner you have your God...patient, loving, merciful. Certainly he would cut you some slack in a situation like that. In the other corner you have the Babylonians...egocentric, merciless, violent—those who slaughtered your family and destroyed your hometown. What are the odds they're going to change the rules because of your religious preference? They're committed to erasing this preference from the face of the earth.

Either way, Daniel had to choose. He had to commit himself to one side or the other. Either he would cheat God of the devotion he deserved or cheat the Babylonians of the cooperation they demanded.

Isn't it interesting that when we look at Daniel's situation, the right thing to do is clear to us? And because we know how the story turned out, we applaud his courage. In fact, this is the kind of story we want our children to read and to learn from. We would consider ourselves successful parents if our teenagers had that kind of courage in the face of temptation. If you're a Christian, chances are this is a story you've read to your children. In your own way you've said to your kids, "Be like Daniel. Do the right thing even when it costs you something."

But when we look at our circumstances, we lose sight. Somehow our situations are different. In fact, you may be arguing with me even now.

"It's not that simple."

"You're not making a fair comparison."

"My circumstances are different."

"That was then; this is now."

"I'm not Daniel!"

Maybe you're right. Maybe your circumstances are too difficult for God. Maybe you should get a special permission slip. After all, Daniel's life was on the line. And what's at stake for you is far more critical than that. If you were to side with your family and let the chips fall where they may at the office, they might…well, you could lose…who knows what the consequences might be? And that's the point. Who knows what would happen? You think you do. But you're only guessing. And besides, God may want to do something unusual. But now I'm getting ahead of myself.

A QUESTION OF LOYALTY

Daniel's choice of diet was an indication of where he placed his loyalty. For us the chief indicator is time. Daniel's loyalty was tested by what he ate. Ours is tested by what we put on our calendars. Where you spend your time is an indication of where your loyalties lie. In effect, you pledge your allegiance to the person or thing that receives your time.

We don't generally associate time with loyalty when it comes to self-evaluation. We make the connection when we evaluate other people, but not ourselves. If someone refuses to give you time, you make a judgment about his or her commitment to you. But we evaluate our own sense of loyalty differently. We judge our loyalties by how we *feel*.

If I were to ask you how loyal you were to your family, you would answer in extreme terms. If I ask for evidence of your loyalty, chances are your answer would not center on the amount of time you spend with them. You would talk about how you felt, what you've done, how far you would go to protect them, provide for them, and so forth. All of this is evidence of how you feel toward your loved ones.

But the chief indicator from your family's perspective is different. It boils down to time. The problem is, your employer or client judges your loyalty in the same way: time. And there's not enough time to go around. So, similar to the story of Daniel, there's a choice to make. Daniel couldn't eat without eating the king's required rations. And if you're like most people, you cannot give all the time expected or required of you to both work and family. Somebody's going to get cheated.

FAITHFUL WHEN FAITHLESS

As you may remember, Daniel decided to disappoint the visible king and cast his fate with the Invisible King, the One who hadn't done much for him lately. He decided to remain faithful despite God's seeming unfaithfulness.

> But Daniel resolved not to defile himself with the royal
> food and wine. (Daniel 1:8)

This is how lasting change begins. It begins with a decision. Before Daniel knew the outcome of his decision, before he understood how he would address the issue with his supervisors, he made up his mind. He decided, regardless of the outcome, "I will not abandon my allegiance to my Invisible King."

Don't rush by this. Whenever I talk to men and women about redirected priorities, they always respond the same way: "But if I do that..." Then they proceed to tell me the future. Suddenly they become fortune-tellers. They tell me what will happen at work, what will happen to their bonuses, what will happen to their reputations. It's amazing the clarity they have about future events. I'm being facetious, of course. But they speak with such authority I'm always tempted to ask for stock advice while they're peering into their crystal balls.

Once they finish telling me what they're sure will happen, they tackle the next tier, the "what abouts":

- What about the kids' college?
- What about our financial goals?
- What about the mortgage?

That's when I pull out my crystal ball and say, "If something doesn't change, you aren't going to need to worry about retirement because you aren't going to retire together anyway. Furthermore, your kids' college fund is going to be used up paying attorneys' fees. And instead of worrying about how to pay the mortgage, you need to decide which one of you will assume it when you aren't living together anymore."

You see, this principle cuts both ways. There's a price to pay either way you go. But for some reason we only look into the future through one set of lenses. And then when our misprioritizing comes home to roost, we wonder what happened.

LOOKING AHEAD

I'm sure Daniel had an inkling of what would happen if he sided against the visible king. But he didn't let that stop him. And once his mind was made up, he came up with a plan. A terrible plan. An unreasonable plan. Get this: he decided to ask his captors if they would change the rules for him!

And he asked the chief official for permission not to
defile himself this way. (Daniel 1:8)

Can you imagine?

There's a familiar scene from the musical *Oliver!* that cap-
tures the absurdity of Daniel's presumption. If you've seen the
movie, you'll no doubt remember it. Oliver, the little orphan
boy, sheepishly approaches the cruel master of the orphanage
with his empty bowl and utters, "Please, sir, I want some more."
The dining hall is silent as every other orphan watches in
amazement. Nobody asks for more. What was he thinking?
And sure enough, the orphanage master lets loose his rage on
the poor orphan child who didn't know any better than to ask
for seconds.

Why would Daniel make such a ridiculous request? Probably because he didn't have any choice. He'd made up his mind.
He might as well see if anybody would go along with him. But
what were the chances that his captors would bend the rules
for him? Humanly speaking, none. Zero. But that's where the
story takes an interesting twist, one that Daniel hadn't necessarily counted on, but one he knew was a distinct possibility.

Now God had caused the official to show favor and
compassion to Daniel. (Daniel 1:9)

The "now God" factor changed everything. What on the surface looked like an impossibility became a reality. Not because of Daniel's wit and insight, but because God decided to honor Daniel for where he placed his loyalty. God's "now" and our "now" are never in sync. I'm sure Daniel would have preferred that God not wait until the last minute to intervene. Things would have been much less stressful if the official had come to him first and suggested a different diet. But that's usually not God's way.

Apart from "now God," it was clear to all those looking on what Daniel's fate would be. As you evaluate the notion of re-prioritizing your time, you're probably faced with some dark realities as well. This is why most of us, once we're to the edge of the precipice, turn around and retreat to what we know.

I tried my hand at surfing once. Everything went well until the moment when I had to stand up on the board. Peering down over the edge of the wave sapped my courage. I felt like I was looking down from the top of a building. Time after time I tried to muster the courage to stand, and every time I retreated from the challenge. It looked so easy from the shore. But I just couldn't commit. The unknown was terrifying.

So it is with those of us who have grown comfortable with the lives we've created for ourselves in the marketplace. Though we consider ourselves risktakers, the fact is, we cower at the prospect of saying no to lucrative opportunities. We're scared to death to leave early. The idea of losing a sale over an extra couple of hours at home causes us to cringe. So we paddle our way to the edge of the wave, take one look, and retreat to what we know, to what we can control.

There would have been no "now God" moment for Daniel had he not made up his mind and charged ahead. There'll be no "now God" moment for you, either, until you place your loyalty where it belongs and give him an opportunity to intervene on your behalf. And the tragedy is, you'll live your entire life and never know what God would have done in response to your faith in him.

This Is a Test

In spite of the official's fondness for Daniel, there were factors that limited what he could do on his Jewish friend's behalf.

> Now God had caused the official to show favor and compassion to Daniel, but the official told Daniel, "I am afraid of my lord the king, who has assigned your food and drink. Why should he see you looking worse than the other young men your age? The king would then have my head because of you." (Daniel 1:9–10)

When Daniel realized that his request put the king's official in danger, he suggested a compromise, a test of sorts:

> Daniel then said to the guard whom the chief official had appointed over Daniel, Hananiah, Mishael and Azariah, "Please test your servants for ten days: Give us nothing but vegetables to eat and water to drink. Then compare our appearance with that of the young men who eat the royal food, and treat your servants in accordance with what you see." So he agreed to this and tested them for ten days. (Daniel 1:11–14)

Daniel wasn't insensitive to the predicament his unusual standards created for his new friend. So he approached the situation diplomatically. He gave the official an out. But he didn't agree to compromise his convictions if the outcome of the test didn't suit the official. If you attended Sunday school as a child, you probably remember what happened next:

> At the end of the ten days they looked healthier and better nourished than any of the young men who ate the royal food. So the guard took away their choice food and the wine they were to drink and gave them vegetables instead.
>
> To these four young men God gave knowledge and

understanding of all kinds of literature and learning. And Daniel could understand visions and dreams of all kinds.

At the end of the time set by the king to bring them into his service, the chief official presented them to Nebuchadnezzar. The king talked with them, and he found none equal to Daniel, Hananiah, Mishael and Azariah; so they entered the king's service. In every matter of wisdom and understanding about which the king questioned them, he found them ten times better than all the magicians and enchanters in his whole kingdom. (Daniel 1:15–20)

Basically, Daniel and his friends got a promotion and a raise.

If you're ready to redirect your priorities, three things are probably going to be required. I say "probably" because I think this narrative is an illustration, not a blueprint.

First, you've got to *make up your mind.* You've got to decide to quit cheating at home before you know how you're going to pull it off, before you know how things are going to sort themselves out.

Second, once you've made up your mind, you need to *come up with a plan*—an exit strategy from your current schedule—and present it to your employer. And, like Daniel's request, your request may appear absolutely ridiculous. But that's only because you don't know what God may want to do on your behalf.

Third, like Daniel, you need to *set up a test*—a trial for the plan.

In the remaining chapters we'll look at each of these steps in detail.

SEVEN

Make Up Your Mind

hoosing not to cheat at home begins with a decision. A decision to quit cheating.

You can't wait until you know how the story is going to end. You can't wait until all the details have been worked out.

You can't wait until another job comes along that doesn't demand such an arduous travel schedule. The decision to stop cheating must precede all of that.

Daniel didn't discover a weak spot in the Babylonian chain of command and exploit it. He made up his mind. Daniel didn't know *how*. He didn't know the *where* or *when*. But he knew the *what*. He made up his mind from the beginning that he wouldn't defile himself, regardless of the outcome.

That's important. As the verses that follow explain, there would be other things Daniel did too. There would be negotiations with the Babylonian authorities and discussions to work out the details. Any gaps would be filled in along the way. But all of that came later. In the beginning there was only Daniel and his decision to take from Nebuchadnezzar and give to God.

JUST IMAGINE

I realize I've already made this point in at least four other chapters. But this is the sticking point. Once you get by this, the rest is…well, it's all hard. But either way, you can't start exploring future possibilities until you have made up your mind.

The temptation is to substitute a condition for a commitment.

"When I…"

"If they…"

I've never seen that work. You may be the exception. If so, write me, and tell me about it. Before you commit to a conditional decision (if that even makes sense), gather your family members together and explain it to them. Look 'em directly in the eyes and say, "You're so important to me that if such and such happens, I'm going to give you more of my undivided time and attention." Then clarify it for them. Say, "You see, such and such is *more important* than you are. So unless such and such happens, I'll have to remain on my present course."

You get the point. Once you make your commitment conditional, you've just underscored the fact that your spouse and the kids really aren't the priority after all. How would you feel if your daughter came home and said she was committed to staying a virgin as long as she got asked to the prom? What kind of commitment is that? What if your son told you he was committed to never cheat on an exam as long as he knew all the answers? Okay, maybe these are unfair comparisons. But in terms of emotional impact, I'm not as far off as you might think.

Now imagine this scenario. Imagine sitting down with your family, looking each one in the eyes, and saying, "Mommy hasn't been home as much as she should. I'm committed to changing that. I'm not sure how just yet. But things are going to change. And they're going to change quickly. You're more important to me than anything or anybody else in the world."

Powerful, huh? And I bet that's genuinely the way you feel. So let's put some feet on it. Commit.

That was the first step for Daniel, and it's the first step for you and me. It all begins with a decision—before you know how the details are going to work out. You may not know how your boss is going to react. You can't predict what will happen financially or with your position at work. But in spite of the uncertainty, you can make up your mind not to cheat your spouse or your family any longer, no matter what. End of conversation.

PREFERENCE VERSUS CONVICTION

Now, I know I'm a preacher. And it's easy for men and women in the business community to excuse themselves from a discussion facilitated by someone who clearly doesn't understand the complexities of his work environment. But for future reference, when was the last time you heard about someone in business going into the ministry because the business environment was too stressful? I'm not looking for sympathy. I just don't want to give you any wiggle room in light of what I'm about to say.

Reprioritizing your world around your family is not just a good idea; it's a God idea. As a Christian, I don't think I have any options when it comes to establishing my priorities. To ask my family to take the leftovers is more than insensitive. It flies in the face of everything we're taught in the New Testament about the family.

Nowhere in Scripture are you commanded to lay down your life for your stock options. Or to love your career like Christ loved the church. We're instructed to *do* our jobs and *love* our families (see Colossians 3:23). When you *love* your job and *do* your family, you've not only stepped outside the bounds of family life, you've stepped outside the will of God.

You can't take the scriptural admonitions concerning marriage seriously without prioritizing your relationships at home over work. It's impossible. As my dad is fond of saying, "God doesn't reveal his will for our consideration. He reveals it for our participation." From God's point of view, this is not a helpful option. This is an imperative. It's part of God's plan for you as a parent and a spouse. Obedience in this area opens you up to the blessings and faithfulness of God at home and at work.

As the story of Daniel reiterates, there's something about an all-or-nothing conviction that activates the divinely driven forces of the universe on your behalf. Following the principles of God results in the blessings of God.

THE AFTERMATH

On the human side of the equation, there are two big benefits to making up your mind in the face of uncertainty.

#1: Momentum
Conviction is essential. Only something as powerful as a heartfelt conviction could reverse the misdirected momentum caused by your misprioritization. The wheels are turning. The ball is

rolling. The problem is, everything's moving in the wrong direction. You have momentum, but it's taking you further and further away from your goal. How do you stop that? How do you turn it around?

You make up your mind.

Conviction is like a bat in the hands of Albert Pujols. A 90-miles-per-hour fastball moving in the direction of the catcher is suddenly transformed into a 120-miles-per-hour rocket headed into center field.

You need something to reverse your momentum. A conviction has the power to do just that.

Let's face it; our world is resistant to change. Old habits die hard. Chances are, there will be significant changes necessary to neutralize the friction between work and family in your life. It's amazing how change resistant your world can become the minute you set out to break the molds. So you'll need all the momentum you can get.

There'll be obstacles to overcome and problems to solve. From where you sit now, you can't fully anticipate the challenges or their solutions. But you can resolve to maintain an unwavering stance when it comes to your priorities. And when the dark clouds of uncertainty come and there are no answers for the moment, your momentum might turn out to be the one thing that carries you through to the other side.

It's a simple matter of physics. When you're going up against an obstacle bigger than you are, momentum is the only equalizer. What you can't muster in terms of mass, you can make up for in velocity. And that could be the deciding factor between success at work and home, or compromise in both places.

#2: Focus

A firmly held conviction sharpens your focus.

When you commit to a direction, it narrows your options. And that in turn forces you to focus only on the options that will lead to the desired results. The reason Daniel proposed an alternative diet is because it was his only option, given his conviction. When you eliminate certain options, it's amazing how resourceful you become. Conviction eliminates options.

When Hernando Cortez landed at Veracruz, Mexico, on April 21, 1519, he ordered the ships in his fleet to be burned. His reason? His goal—his *conviction*—was to conquer Mexico for Spain. He knew he and his men would face many obstacles. They would be forced to confront Aztec, Cuban, and Mayan warriors. As long as there were ships to retreat to, retreat would remain an option. But retreat wasn't an option for Cortez. His conviction, and his decision to burn the ships, eliminated at least one option. That symbolic gesture rallied his troops to focus all their resources on achieving victory. In an amazingly short amount of time, Mexico was theirs.

Making up your mind not to cheat your family anymore is

a decision. Interestingly, the Latin root for the word *decidere* means "to cut off." Deciding not to cheat at home involves "cutting off" those behaviors and habits that are contrary to your new conviction. Making up your mind isn't just about choosing an option. That's only half the story. It's also about thoroughly eliminating all competing options. Choosing results in focus.

Eliminating options is part of what makes this process so painful. Giving up good things for the sake of what's best is not easy, even when we're convinced it's right.

I know for many the prospect of giving up even a portion of the accolades, financial rewards, and emotional strokes associated with the marketplace is extremely difficult. We're always tempted to look for a way around the necessity of missing out on tangible rewards. The lure of recognition keeps many from ever acting on their conviction to go home. But you can't have it both ways. Just as you've missed out on some of the rewards of being what God has called you to be at home, now you must embrace the prospects of missing out in the marketplace.

What are you afraid of losing? What will you have a tendency to try to hold on to in spite of your decision to reprioritize? It's important for you to know exactly what that is. Because chances are, that thing, that relationship, that perk, perhaps that hobby, may eventually become the thing God uses to seal your commitment one way or the other. That may be the ship you have to burn. And in burning it, you may send the clearest message you've ever sent to your family about their priority in your life.

THE GIFT

On many occasions I've talked with men who confided that it wasn't their work that was the point of contention in their homes. It was a hobby. For some it was the time they spent at the gym. For others their mistress was the golf course. For one very close friend, it was his bicycle.

In his early twenties, Mike was an Olympic hopeful. He came very close to making the 1988 Olympic team. When I met Mike, he was thirty-seven and continued to compete and to win. Riding through the mountains of northern Georgia was more than an afternoon event. For Mike, it was a passion. It wasn't uncommon for Mike to ride one hundred miles in a weekend.

But riding wasn't a family event. It was time reserved for Mike and his buddies. And it was time that could have and, as Mike later admitted, should have been given to his wife, Angela, and their then eight-year-old daughter.

Like most wives, Angela believed Mike loved her more than his bicycle. But she didn't feel it. She *knew* his heart, but she *felt* his schedule. Mike did everything imaginable to play both sides of the aisle. He offered to take Angela with him on biking weekends. He entered fewer races. But as long as his bicycle hung in the garage, it served as a point of contention. Even when Mike was home on Saturdays, she knew he would rather be out riding. Angela felt like she was competing with rubber and aluminum.

I'll never forget the Sunday afternoon Mike showed up at my house with his mountain bike. "Here," he said. "I want you to have this."

I assumed he wanted me to hold on to it for a while, which I was more than happy to do.

"No," he said. "I'm giving it to you. No more biking."

I was shocked. To begin with, this was a two-thousand-dollar bike. But more than that, I knew Mike's love for biking.

"This is something God has wanted me to do for some time. I thought there was a way around it. But there wasn't," Mike said. "So, here it is. Have fun."

I asked how Angela responded. I was sure she was as surprised as I was. But I had a feeling she felt more than simple surprise. Mike confirmed my suspicion.

"Her heart melted," he said. "She cried when I told her. She told me I didn't need to get rid of it for good. But I insisted. I think she feels more loved by me now than ever before."

Later, Angela said, "I never thought Mike would give it up. Nothing he has ever done has meant more to my daughter and me. I know how much he loved to ride. For him to walk away from his bikes is…well…I feel like we're his priority again."

For Mike, there was a bridge to burn. Giving away his bike removed an option. Now it would be easier for him to focus.

What about you? Are there bridges you need to burn? What are the bridges that making this decision will require you to burn? Are there accounts you need to hand off? Are there some out-of-town meetings that need to be handled on the phone? Is there an offer you need to refuse? A promotion you need to give back? Once you've made up your mind, it will become all too clear what stands in the way of your being able to focus on your commitment to reprioritize.

A STAKE IN THE GROUND

Making up your mind will require some specific commitments. They may appear to be impractical at first. That's okay. We'll discuss how to get from here to there in the next chapter. For now let's be impractical. What exactly are you committing to do? Spending *more* time at home and *less* time at the office isn't specific enough.

The more specific you are about the results you feel called to achieve, the easier it will be to follow through. And the easier it will be for others to hold you accountable.

Daniel was pretty specific: no meat and wine from the king's table. That was his nonnegotiable.

So what's your nonnegotiable? What does it look like? Does it mean leaving the office every day at five thirty, regardless? Does it mean never missing one of your children's performances or ball games? What does this commitment look like in your world?

Again, promising to do "better" won't get it. You've already done that. That terminology doesn't even register with your family. They've heard that before.

I know this is scary. It's easier to be vague. When you're vague, you have the advantage of feeling like you're making progress, but with none of the liabilities of a specific promise. We've all played that game. Everybody feels better for the moment, but nothing changes.

Let's start with this question: What change would your spouse most like you to make in regard to your schedule?

I'll never forget the afternoon I asked Sandra that question. She didn't hesitate. She looked right at me and said, "I would love for you to be home by four every afternoon."

At the time we had two preschoolers and a third child on the way. By four thirty she was done. She'd given all she had to give. When I came stumbling through the door at five thirty or six, she was running on fumes. In that same conversation she informed me that between four and six were the two most difficult hours of the day. If she could change anything about my schedule, she would have me home during those two hours.

Now let me put that conversation in the broader context of my professional life so that you can understand my predicament.

TAKING CARE OF BUSINESS

My little chat with Sandra took place one month after I'd agreed to help pioneer what eventually became North Point Community Church. If you've ever started anything—whether it's a new church or a new business—you know that start-ups of any kind require limitless time, attention, and energy. Our staff was lean, we had few members, money was very tight, and every resource was stretched thin.

Meanwhile, the demands were starting to pile up. And at that point in the life cycle of an organization, you need 100 percent from everybody—especially the leader.

Leaving the office in time to be home by four o'clock seemed like a terrible idea—at least from the standpoint of leading a start-up organization. One thing working in my favor was the fact that our offices were literally ten minutes away from our home. But that still meant leaving a few minutes before four.

As we continued to talk, she agreed that if I left the office at four, it would still make a big difference. As Sandra and I evaluated our whole situation, discussed our schedules, and took an honest look at where we were as a family, it became apparent that if I was committed to making her and the kids feel like my priority, I would have to limit my time at work to forty-five hours a week.

That seemed extreme at the time. I didn't know of any pastor who worked only forty-five hours a week. In fact, I didn't know any professional who had a forty-five-hour workweek. I felt guilty. I felt like I wasn't being a good example to the rest of the staff. And frankly, I wasn't convinced that I could build a church with that kind of schedule.

But that was the commitment I made. Leaving at four o'clock and working a forty-five-hour workweek were my nonnegotiables. I'm not recommending that for anyone else. That's just where we were, and that's what I felt I needed to do.

So in my own way, I made a deal with God. Essentially I said, "Lord, feel free to build whatever kind of church you can build with forty-five hours of my time. You know that's all I have right now."

As a result of my decision, there were meetings that got cut short. There were programs I didn't attend. There were counseling needs that I had to delegate. I was usually the first to leave the office. And I knew my inflexibility frustrated some people.

But it was what I felt I had to do to be what my family needed me to be. I had to cheat somewhere. I decided to cheat at work.

And for me, that meant cheating at church!

LEGACY

In addition to working close to home, there were two things that made this easier for me than it is for most people. First, as a pastor, I was reminded almost every week of what can happen in marriages when husbands or wives cheat their families instead of the marketplace. I'd seen mature Christian men and women fall into the trap of overinvesting at work for the sake of a big payoff down the road. Furthermore, I'd seen way too many pastors sacrifice their families under the guise of doing "the Lord's work" when, in fact, it had little to do with the Lord's work and more to do with propping up their own egos. From the very beginning I knew what could happen if I wasn't intentional about how I divided my time. I've never believed that I was an exception to the rule. I have all the negative potential of any other father, husband, or pastor.

The other advantage I had was growing up in the home of a successful pastor who made his family a priority. My dad was home for dinner. He never missed a basketball game (in spite of the fact that I was on the bench just about as much as he was on the bleachers). We took long family vacations. In fact, when we were on vacation, we never, and I mean never, even went to church!

I could walk into his office at any moment unannounced and be warmly welcomed. I don't know how many hours a week he worked. That's really not important. What's important is that I never felt like I was competing with the church for his time. Family was clearly his priority.

These two things made it easier for me to entrust my career success to God. I've never felt the pressure some feel to build a successful church. My responsibility is to prioritize my life in accordance with the priorities laid out in Scripture. That includes doing my work as unto the Lord and loving my wife as Christ loved the church. In other words, working hard when I'm at work and then going home and forgetting about it.

In the early days, when our church was still an experiment, I had no idea how my schedule would impact progress or morale. What I did know was that we're never called to violate the principles of God in order to attain or maintain the blessings of God. I wanted to be a part of a church that God would be free to bless. I really didn't know exactly what that meant. But I did know that the best way to find out was to order my private world in accordance with his priorities for me as a husband, father, and pastor.

That was more than sixteen years ago. I've never regretted that decision. Our children are all teenagers now. No one requires Sandra's constant attention. She doesn't need me to be home as early anymore. But I'm still one of the first to leave in the afternoon. And I'm almost always home for dinner. And to be honest, it's not because I'm so "committed" to my family. It's because I love to go home.

I feel so strongly about this principle that I encourage our staff to follow suit. "Cheat at work," I tell 'em. "Cheat me. But don't you dare cheat at home."

MAKING A STAND

So, back to you. If you were to ask your spouse and kids what schedule changes they would love to see you make, what would they say? Maybe you should ask. Their answers may be totally impractical, but it won't hurt anything to know. Don't worry about *how*. Focus on *what*. Presume on God for a minute. Assume he's going to support you. Assume for the moment that he'll come through for you, intervene on your behalf. What would your schedule look like? What would have to change?

Now before you panic, I want you to think about something. The things that will make or break you professionally are not related to the number of hours you work. A sixty-hour workweek doesn't guarantee you more success than a forty-five-hour workweek. Even if you're punching a clock, more hours don't result in greater success.

Think about where you are today professionally. Consider your success for just a moment. Are you where you are today as a result of the number of hours you've put in? Is there an actual correlation between how many hours you've worked and the success you've enjoyed? I would venture to guess that your success is the result of opportunities that came your way, lucky breaks, hunches you followed up on, people you met by accident, and risks you decided to take.

When successful men and women reminisce, their defining moments professionally are never related to how many hours they worked. And I've never heard of a business failure attributed to a work schedule. Success is always related to good decisions, unexpected opportunities, market conditions, and a host of other things that nobody really had any control over. The sixty hours you work this week may not reap nearly the same productivity as the sixty hours you put in next week. Why? Because of things you have no control over.

It's important that you associate your professional success with those things that really make a difference. And the length of your workweek doesn't play as significant a role as you might at first think. There are other factors that impact your success more significantly than your schedule. Again, these are things you can't control.

But the opposite is true in family life. Happily married couples never attribute their success to unexpected opportunities, market conditions, luck, or good timing. You've never met a healthy family who chalked up their success to being in the right place at the right time. With family, success is always related to *time*. In the world of family, you have far more control over the things that really make a difference.

This is why it makes so much sense to entrust our careers to our heavenly Father. For only he controls those things that make the most significant difference in our professions. This is why it's safe to ask him to fill the gaps at work when it's time for us to go home.

Don't be afraid to consider a new schedule. Chances are, there's no necessary correlation between your current success and the number of hours you're putting in anyway. The make-or-break events, relationships, market conditions, and closings are usually related to things over which God exercises control.

So make up your mind. And then begin piecing together a plan by which you can make your decision a reality.

EIGHT

Create a Plan

You've made up your mind. You've identified some specific nonnegotiables. You've committed to stand by your convictions. Now what? *What's the best way to get from here to there?* Specifically, how do you go about convincing your employer to lighten up?

In short, very carefully.

Building up a head of steam over your decision to reprioritize could be dangerous. The goal in this exercise is not to lose your job or even to make a point with the folks in your office. The goal is to negotiate your way into a more manageable and flexible schedule. Once again, Daniel provides us with a model to follow. Daniel knew how to be both dogmatic and diplomatic, which isn't always easy to do. He wasn't going to compromise his convictions. But he wasn't going to demand his way either.

It would have been easy for Daniel to take a defiant posture with the Babylonians. But Daniel resisted. He didn't stage a hunger strike or withdraw into passive-aggressive resistance of their authority. Daniel was committed to doing the right thing, the right way. He was dogmatic in his convictions, but not in his approach. He was immovable yet humble, unshakable but sensitive.

WISDOM AND TACT

This unusual ability to maintain his cool in a highly emotional environment surfaces again later in Daniel's tenure under Nebuchadnezzar. Years later the king had a dream that he expected his wise men to recount for him and interpret. Interpreting dreams was one thing. Telling the king what he dreamed was something else entirely. The king lost his patience and decided to execute his entire staff of wise men and magicians. When Daniel heard of the king's edict, he set out to find the commander in charge of carrying out the king's orders. Notice Daniel's approach:

When Arioch, the commander of the king's guard,

had gone out to put to death the wise men of Babylon,

Daniel spoke to him with *wisdom and tact*. (Daniel

2:14, emphasis mine)

"Wisdom and tact." He's hours, perhaps minutes, away from losing his life over something he had nothing to do with, and he's able to approach the commander with wisdom and tact. Desperation and fear I could understand, but not wisdom and tact.

Now before you write Daniel off as just another larger-than-life Bible superhero, you need to know something else about this story. After Daniel's diplomatic discussion with Arioch, he went home and had a different kind of discussion with his buddies.

Here's what happened:

Then Daniel returned to his house and explained the

matter to his friends Hananiah, Mishael and Azariah.

He urged them to plead for mercy from the God of

heaven concerning this mystery, so that he and his

friends might not be executed with the rest of the wise

men of Babylon. (Daniel 2:17–18)

Daniel wasn't completely fearless. He didn't have a death wish. He wasn't above begging God for mercy. He knew that tact and diplomacy weren't enough to get them over this hurdle. They were going to need another "now God" moment to survive.

So what's the lesson in all of this?

God honors diplomacy and dependency. One doesn't supplant the other. Both are necessary. Having a plan isn't a lack of faith. Walking in and giving an ultimatum at work isn't necessarily an expression of faith. You need wisdom, tact, and some friends praying for you back at home.

POSTURING

I belabor this point because I know firsthand how easy it is for the pendulum to swing from one extreme to the other. When we at last catch a glimpse of the hurt we've caused at home, there's something in us that wants to fix things immediately. It's not enough to make up our minds; we want to do something.

But the wrong actions for the right reason produce painful results. You can do the right thing the wrong way and end up in a worse situation than the one you left. The operative word throughout this book has been *choosing*, not *reacting*.

The fact that you've decided to make a change in your life doesn't necessarily mean the folks at work are under any obligation to change. There's no value in punishing your employer.

Your attitude and approach should be seasoned with diplomacy and tact. Besides, the source of your frustration is not your employer. It's the decisions you've made in response to the demands of your employer and the marketplace in general. Nobody forced you to work there. It was your decision. You, not they, must bear the consequences.

No Deception

One other point of clarification needs to be made at this point. "Cheating" at work in the way we've been discussing is simply about reallocating your limited time assets according to your predetermined priorities. It has nothing to do with defrauding your employer or deceiving your employer. As we've said on several occasions, the blessings of God are never attained by violating the principles of God. Daniel didn't secretly abandon the king's diet plan. There was no deceit. He told the official exactly what his intentions were. Then he prepared himself for the consequences.

Depending on your job situation, this approach may call for a great deal of candor with your employer. The more non-confrontational your personality, the more difficult it will be for you to actually approach your boss or supervisor with whatever plan you come up with. You may be tempted to simply start cutting out early, leaving her with a false impression, living with the hope that she doesn't discover that you aren't around as much. But that's not what we're suggesting.

THE PLAN

Buried in the interaction between Daniel and the king's official is the framework for a transition strategy that can be lifted out of its original context and applied in our modern culture.

For the remainder of this chapter, we'll examine the three components that serve as the outline for Daniel's course of action. If you work for yourself or are in a position where you set your own hours, steps one and two may not be relevant for your situation. But don't skip the third step.

I really don't like lists. Life doesn't happen according to any list I've ever read. And I've never mastered anything by following a list. Furthermore, I don't think Daniel was following a prescribed method in his attempt to broker a deal with the king's official. So, I don't view these three elements as a prescription that must be followed. But as you think through how you'll approach those in authority over you at the office, you would do well to consider Daniel's strategy.

Essentially, Daniel did three things:

1. He asked for permission to change his work conditions.

2. He listened to the objections from his supervisor.
3. He proposed a test that took into account his supervisor's concerns.

DANIEL ASKED

And he [Daniel] asked the chief official for permission not to defile himself this way. (Daniel 1:8)

The first thing Daniel did was go right to the person in charge and address the issue head-on. He didn't attempt to deceive the king's official. He didn't stage a hunger strike. He went right up and asked to be an exception to the rule.

He didn't demand. He asked. He didn't ask with the assumption that his personal conviction would carry any weight with the king's official. What was imperative for him was certainly not imperative for everyone else. In addition, Daniel offered an alternative. He didn't simply tell the king's official what he didn't want to eat. He suggested a substitute diet.

If you're in a position where you aren't free to adjust your schedule without running it by someone first, Daniel's approach has a lot of merit:

- Address the issue directly.
- Ask; don't demand.
- Offer alternatives.

When I challenge men and women to address this issue with their supervisors, I receive varying responses—everything from, "She'll probably understand" to "He's liable to let me go right then and there." Chances are, your anticipated response falls somewhere between those two. If you don't expect to get much support from your boss or supervisor, you may be tempted to avoid this step altogether. That would probably be a big mistake.

Addressing the issue directly accomplishes three things. It allows you to discover how serious you are about your decision. It gives you an opportunity to find out if you're operating under false assumptions about your employer. Your boss may be more open than you suspect. Most important, addressing the issue directly gives your heavenly Father an opportunity to work on your behalf. If you fail to address your schedule directly, you may be inclined to deceive your employer. Being direct will help you avoid that temptation.

Ask; don't demand. Even if you're ready to walk, just ask. When you ask, you underscore your supervisor's authority. When you demand, you undermine his or her authority. Don't include an ultimatum with your request. An ultimatum will put your supervisor on the defensive. It's very important for bosses to feel like they're making decisions rather than responding to threats. People will knowingly make bad decisions just to save face when they're threatened.

Offer alternatives. You can anticipate what some of the concerns will be. You know some of what your supervisor will feel like he or she is giving up by allowing you to adjust your schedule. Address those losses. Chances are, if your boss knows you've thought the issue through from his perspective, he won't feel as if he has to defend anything. Do your best to give back more than you're taking away.

If the answer's no, just thank the boss for his time and go back to work. Now's not the time to communicate your inflexibility on this issue. Wait. Give God an opportunity to work. As an employer, I know there have been many occasions that I've said no to a request and then changed my mind the next day, once I had an opportunity to think about it.

DANIEL LISTENED

The commander of the officials said to Daniel, "I am afraid of my lord the king, who has appointed your food and your drink; for why should he see your faces looking more haggard than the youths who are your own age? Then you would make me forfeit my head to the king." (Daniel 1:10, NASB)

Once Daniel had taken his idea public, he *listened*. And when he did, he discovered some extremely valuable information.

He found out that the king's official was open to altering the meal plan. The issue wasn't what Daniel ate; it was how he looked and performed. So Daniel went to work on addressing the official's primary concern. We'll return to this topic later.

Chances are, you're pretty confident you know what your employer's concerns will be. But of the three or four things mentioned, most likely, one of them will be his chief concern. Listen with the goal of identifying the issue that makes your supervisor most uncomfortable with your proposal. Where exactly do the fingernails hit the chalkboard?

Don't argue. Don't confront. Ask lots of questions. Ask for clarification. Dig. Discover. Empathize. Take notes. Nod. Agree. And then leave! If possible, leave before you hear no. When all the issues are on the table and you think you may have a bead on the one or two primary concerns, get up and go. End the conversation with something along the lines of, "I see how this request might cause a problem. If I were you, I would be concerned about that (once you've discerned what "that" is) as well. The last thing I want to do is hurt the company or embarrass you in any way. If it's all right with you, I would like to think about what you've said and get back with you."

If the answer wasn't yes, you have to go back, so do what you can to keep the door cracked.

NINE

Set Up a Test

W e've seen how Daniel (1) asked for permission to change his work conditions, then (2) listened to objections from his supervisor.

Now let's get to the third step in Daniel's strategy.

DANIEL PROPOSED A TEST

With his plan settled in his mind, Daniel came before the overseer and proposed a test that would take into account his supervisor's concerns:

Please test your servants for ten days.... Then let our
appearance be observed in your presence and the
appearance of the youths who are eating the king's
choice food; and deal with your servants according
to what you see. (Daniel 1:12–13, NASB)

Once Daniel identified the official's chief concern, he went
back and proposed a test. Since performance rather than diet
was the issue, he figured the thing to do was to challenge the
king's official to scrutinize his performance.

Notice how he closes his proposal:

And deal with your servants according to what you see.
(1:13, NASB)

Once again, he never threatened the official's authority or
control. Still, there was no ultimatum. By committing to a ten-
day trial, Daniel's overseer had virtually little to lose. How sick
could Daniel become in just ten days? Certainly any sign of
diet-related frailty in such a short period could be easily re-
versed. Furthermore, it's assumed that he could have stopped
the experiment at just one or two days if he changed his mind.

Here's where you have something in common with Daniel.
His overseer's primary concern was performance, not diet.
That's your employer's primary concern as well. The real issue

is not the number of hours we spend in the office; it's productivity that matters. Without knowing what you do for a living, I would wager that there are several factors that affect your productivity as much as, or more than, time. Knowing what these are works to your advantage.

The next step for you, whether you report directly to someone else or not, is to set up a trial. A trial is disarming. If anyone has objections, a well-designed trial will usually isolate those concerns and neutralize them. How much can go wrong in just thirty days? Besides, you're inviting your boss to scrutinize your productivity. How many people have walked into his office in the past six months and asked for closer supervision and additional evaluation?

A trial is not a compromise. It's not a watered-down version of your original conviction. Daniel didn't compromise his standard. He devised a way for the king's official to see firsthand that he could alter his diet without reducing his productivity. The test was merely a tool through which to demonstrate his point.

You see, the kind of cheating at work we've been discussing isn't really cheating at all. It's merely testing to see how well the requirements of your job can be met under a different arrangement. Odds are, your performance will improve. I say that based on the testimonies of those who have taken this challenge. What's initially viewed as a self-serving concession that benefits only you may, in fact, turn out to benefit the entire company.

I mentioned earlier that if you're in control of your schedule, you should seriously consider making this step. Set up a trial. Tell your family what you intend to do. Establish an objective way to measure your productivity. Set a time limit, preferably thirty days, and stick with your schedule. Come home on time. Limit your travel.

This is far more effective than telling yourself, "I'm going to do better."

You'll be far more motivated to be consistent for a prescribed period of time than you will if you make a commitment to change forever. Instead of a "from now on" promise, just make a "for the next thirty days" promise. That's measurable. That's something you can stay focused on.

You need to do this for your sake. You need to see what God is willing to do on your behalf if you'll simply trust him. When you do a trial, you'll be watching with greater intensity. You'll pay better attention to detail. You'll know if it's working.

THE INTERVENTION

At the end of ten days their appearance seemed better
and they were fatter than all the youths who had been
eating the king's choice food. So the overseer continued

to withhold their choice food and the wine they were to
drink, and kept giving them vegetables.

As for these four youths, God gave them knowledge
and intelligence in every branch of literature and wisdom; Daniel even understood all kinds of visions and
dreams. (Daniel 1:15–17, NASB)

One can't help but wonder what Daniel would have done if
the test hadn't gone in his favor. Was there a plan B? Would
Daniel have proposed a different test? Would he have appealed
directly to the king?

We don't know.

But every indication is that Daniel had no intention of
shrinking from his original decision. He would remain committed to his priorities, regardless of the outcome of the trial.
But don't you know he was doing everything in his power to
outperform his peers during those critical ten days! And it
worked. His alternative diet enhanced his performance.

The text, however, indicates that something divine happened. Daniel and his friends didn't merely outsmart their peers.
They weren't simply the benefactors of a healthy diet. Verse 17
says, "God gave them knowledge and intelligence." They were
the recipients of divine intervention. Not a miracle per se; there
was nothing observably supernatural about what happened, but
there was certainly something special about those Israelite boys.

Through the years I've challenged hundreds of men and women to follow Daniel's example. Again and again those who have taken me up on the challenge come back with remarkable stories to tell. Stories that often border on the supernatural; events that hint of divine intervention:

"I get more work done in less time."

"An opportunity dropped in my lap out of nowhere."

"A deal I assumed was dead suddenly sprang back to life."

"I have more business than I can keep up with."

And that's just on the business side. On the domestic front, things are always better as well. Men, especially, talk about how much more they enjoy going home. As one fellow expressed it, "I feel like my wife is actually happy to see me."

You'll never know what God is willing to do on your behalf until you're willing to step out and to trust him. When your obedience intersects with his faithfulness, you'll sense his divine presence. You'll experience the intervention of the Father.

God honors those who honor him. Honor him at home and experience his blessing there. Honor him in the marketplace and look for him to show up there as well.

God is no stranger to the marketplace. He created economics. He understands values. There are more verses in the Bible about money than about heaven and hell combined. He's as capable of intervening in your office on Monday afternoon as he is in your church on Sunday morning. Because your work is important to you, it's important to him—because you're important to him.

Position yourself to be blessed by conducting your business in a way that invites God into the mix. Determine a schedule that honors your employer and your family. If necessary, present your ideas to your boss. Conduct a trial. And then watch to see what God does on your behalf.

———∿———

TEN

Trading Places

In the real world there are few fairy-tale endings. This whole process may continue to seem out of reach from where you sit. Even Daniel's story may be a little too "and they all lived happily ever after" for you. That's understandable. In a highly competitive market, the odds are against you being cut much slack. So it seems appropriate to end our time together with a story about a friend of mine who got no for an answer.

I've known Grant for over twenty years. He's been a mentor as well as a friend. Grant is sixty-four and has four incredible kids, nine fine grandkids, and a marriage that most couples would die for. Early in our friendship I asked Grant to tell me how he ended up working for himself. The story that followed is one that I've told many times. And it has given me courage at several critical junctions in my own journey.

When he was in his early twenties, Grant went to work for a fellow in the outdoor advertising business. Basically, they built and sold advertisements on billboards. Now Grant's the kind of guy who could sell just about anything to anybody. So he did quite well in the outdoor advertising business. One thing led to another, and before long Grant was making a lot of money for a kid his age. Furthermore, the owner, Tom, promised Grant a cut of the profits if he ever sold the business, which he eventually did. But there was a problem.

Tom expected his employees to work six days a week. He lived for his business, and he figured everybody else ought to as well. If you weren't in the office Monday through Saturday, there was something wrong. You weren't a company man. Whenever anyone in the inner circle griped, Tom reminded him or her of the big payoff down the road.

Now Grant didn't mind working hard. And he certainly didn't mind being well compensated for his labor. But at that time, he and Patty and his two "young-uns," as he referred to them, didn't see eye to eye with Tom when it came to prioritizing business and family. Grant and Patty had a vision for their family that went beyond owning a big house and a couple of new cars. And working every Saturday pretty much eliminated any hopes of creating the family environment they were envisioning.

So Grant made up his mind to forgo this "excellent" opportunity. As he tells the story, "Me and Patty sat down and decided that this was not the way we were going to raise our family. So I decided to offer Tom an alternative schedule, and if he couldn't accept that, we would just have to find something else to do."

As it turned out, Tom wasn't open to Grant's suggestion. But as Grant found out later, Tom didn't think he had the nerve to just walk out. When Grant turned in his resignation, Tom grinned and asked Grant what he was going to do. Grant told him he didn't know—and he didn't. But he knew one thing: whatever he found to do next, it would *support* rather than compete with what he envisioned for his family. In Grant's words, "I told Tom I would let him determine my exit strategy and that I would do everything I could to ensure a smooth transition. I don't think he thought I was serious. He knew I couldn't go anywhere else and make that kind of money. And I wasn't sure I could either." So after a couple of awkward weeks in the office, Grant and Patty loaded up the station wagon with everything they could carry and headed out of town.

Now I'm tempted not to tell you the rest of the story. The

reason being, it's really not important. The point is, Grant decided to quit cheating at home. And now, these many years later, he looks back at that decision and considers it a defining moment, not so much in terms of his career, but in terms of what happened to his family. Grant didn't know what would happen financially. But he knew what he couldn't continue to allow to happen in his family.

Grant went on to begin his own outdoor company in a different part of the country. God blessed his courage and commitment. His businesses have thrived. But more important, he and his wife saw their vision for their children become a reality.

As I mentioned, his former employer did finally sell his company. The men who stayed with him all those years received big checks. But most of them had lost their families along the way. A couple of them declared bankruptcy a few years after they received their compensation. The owner of the company paid a price relationally as well. His children are grown and gone. His interaction with them is infrequent and superficial.

Looking back, Grant has no doubt that God intervened on his behalf. "My conviction about working six days a week was the thing God used to get us out of that situation," he said. This was his "now God" moment. It wasn't a miracle in the supernatural sense. But it was clearly God's tangible faithfulness in the life of a couple who was committed to doing things right.

THE REST OF THE STORY

I introduced you to Joel Manby in chapter 1. He experienced a
"now God" moment as well.

When we left off, Joel had just made up his mind to stop
cheating at home. He sat down with his wife, Marki, and identified several nonnegotiables. He would limit travel to one night
a week—a criteria that seemed unrealistic if he was going to
function as a CEO. In addition, they established a weekly date
night. Joel determined to be home in time to put his daughters
to bed each night. And he would stop working on Sundays.

As Joel reviewed the changes he would need to make, it
became apparent that he was going to need to make a job
change. The Internet company had stayed afloat, but the work
load was even more demanding. He knew it was pointless to
even discuss these kinds of issues with his current employer. His
only option was to start looking for another opportunity.

Because of his background and education, Joel was confident that he could find another job. The challenge would be
finding a company that would allow him the flexibility he needed
in order to accomplish what he desperately needed to accomplish at home.

A few days after he'd determined to make a change, Joel
received a call from an old friend. Jack Herschend, a Christian,
was the owner of Herschend Family Entertainment, a small

entertainment company in Atlanta. Joel had served on the board in the past but had never considered the company a prospect for his own employment. The entertainment industry wasn't even on his radar at this time. When Jack asked Joel how things were going, it was as if he opened a floodgate. As Joel shared the details of his dilemma, the tears began to flow. Jack listened as Joel described the changes he needed to make and the challenge of finding employment that would afford him that kind of flexibility.

Then Jack said something that Joel never expected: "Well, it's funny you mentioned that. As you know, I'm retiring in November. The purpose of my call was to see if you would be open to serving as chairman of our company. I've hesitated for some time to contact you about this, because frankly, I just didn't think this would be something you would be open to."

As Jack began to describe the job, Joel thought it sounded like the perfect solution. The company was domestic, not international. It was private, not public. Travel would be limited.

There was just one problem. The salary was about 30 percent below what Joel needed in order to reach his financial goals.

But God wasn't finished yet.

Jack suggested they pray together right there on the phone. By now, Joel was in his parking space at work. So he listened while Jack asked God to give Joel something part-time to help bridge the gap to allow Joel to make the job change. Jack specifically asked God for something like a board seat with a company that would pay the extra 30 percent.

Joel hung up the phone, walked into his office, and sat down at the desk to start his day. Just then, the phone rang. It was a recruiter wanting to know if Joel might be interested in a board seat for a company based in Memphis. The pay was almost exactly the 30 percent Joel needed to bridge the gap. "I'd never had anything like that happen in my life! It sent chills up my spine. I called Marki, and we both cried as we reflected on God's faithfulness to our family."

Within a couple of months, Joel had made the transition. "For the first time in years, I had peace in my life. My marriage was healthier. My kids were happier. I renewed my friendships. I didn't have to miss church. Things were better than they'd ever been."

Now, over ten years later, Joel and Marki are raising *four* beautiful daughters, having adopted a daughter from China. Joel has transitioned into president and CEO of HFE, which is an award-winning industry leader in family entertainment with over twenty-five properties.

ALL IN A DAY'S WORK

Joel's and Grant's stories aren't as unusual as you might think. I don't believe for a minute that God guarantees us a salary upgrade if we obey him. But I do know that God honors those who place their faith in him. Jesus summarized it this way:

> Seek first His kingdom and His righteousness, and all
> these things will be added to you. (Matthew 6:33, NASB)

In other words, order your world around your heavenly Father's priorities and then trust him to fill the gaps created by your faithfulness. Instead of asking God to stand watch over your family while you give to your career what belongs at home, turn the prayer around. Go home, seek him first, and ask him to bless things at work. In time you'll discover that when you prioritize correctly at work and home, God will honor you in *both* arenas. Everybody wins.

MISPLACED LOYALTY

Let's face it. One day you'll come home from the office for the last time. Nobody retires from his or her family to spend his or her final days in the office. Your last day may be at sixty-five when you retire or at thirty-five when you're laid off. Either way, you're coming home. What and who you come home to will be determined by how you live out your priorities between now and then.

If you're like most people, one person stands between you and the end of your current employment. Tomorrow you could be called into someone's office and told that your services aren't needed anymore. Perhaps a decision like that would require the vote of a board. Either way, somebody has the power to send you home with the contents of your office in the trunk of your car.

I've seen too many men and women cheat their families only to find that the companies they worked for weren't nearly as loyal to them as they were to the companies.

Loyalty in the marketplace is rarely reciprocated. It's sad when men or women are forced out of organizations they bled for to return home to the families they've neglected.

Why give your ultimate loyalty to an organization where your value is conditional upon your ability to perform? Why betray those whose loyalty is unconditional? Why devote so much of yourself to something you know you'll leave, and so little time to those you'll eventually come home to? It doesn't make sense, does it? Yet without a conscious decision to do otherwise, that's exactly what most of us are prone to do.

THE THIRTY-DAY CHALLENGE

In closing, I want to urge you to take the thirty-day challenge. Make up your mind not to cheat at home for thirty days. Mark it on your calendar. Sit down with your spouse and determine exactly what that will look like. And then start!

Instead of leaving the office when you're finished with everything, leave in time to get home when you've committed to be home. For thirty days say no to anything that has the potential to pull you away from your decision. Decide now to say no at those times. In doing so, you place your career and finances squarely in the capable hands of your heavenly Father.

As you drive away from the office, ask God to fill the gaps at the office while you attend to your unique responsibilities at home. At the end of thirty days, sit down and evaluate what has happened at home, in your finances, and to your productivity at work. You'll be surprised.

Don't cheat the people who love you most. Don't cheat the person who's looking forward to spending the rest of his or her life with you. Don't cheat yourself of the peace that comes with knowing you're squarely in the will of the One who created you. Don't cheat your kids of the security that comes with knowing that they're Mommy and Daddy's priorities.

It has been said before. It's worth saying again. Nobody gets to the end of his life and wishes he'd spent more time at the office. You won't be the first.

Make up your mind.

Develop a plan.

Deliver it diplomatically.

Be willing to walk.

And then watch for God.

After all, he takes full responsibility for the life that's wholly devoted to him.

DISCUSSION QUESTIONS

U se the following questions to help you get the most from this book and to apply what you learn to your life.

If you're part of a group that's going through this book and meeting weekly to discuss it, you may want to structure a four-week course as follows:

Week One: Introduction and Chapters 1 and 2

Week Two: Chapters 3, 4, and 5

Week Three: Chapters 6 and 7

Week Four: Chapters 8, 9, and 10

Or, for a slower pace, you can simply read and discuss one chapter each week.

WEEK ONE

Introduction: Everybody Cheats

1. What are some typical examples in your life of how you decide to give up one thing in order to gain something else?

2. In what ways do you most often experience the tension between work and family? In what situations does this tension seem most intense?

3. What do you expect to gain from going through this book?

Chapter 1: When Your World Needs Reordering

4. In what ways can you relate to Joel and Marki's story?

5. In your understanding, how is Andy using the term *cheating* as it relates to tensions between work and family?

    How do you see this relating to your own situation?

6. Andy says our problem in this area is neither discipline nor organization; instead, he says, it's a matter of too little time available and our need therefore to prioritize. How much would you say this conclusion matches your own situation?

Chapter 2: Collision Course

7. Andy writes, "Both work and family originate with the same Source: God. He created them to peacefully coexist. The tension between the two is understand-

able, but not unavoidable." How fully do you agree
with Andy's assessment?

What are the implications of this assessment for
your own life, as you seek to balance work and family
responsibilities?

8. When it comes to work, what attitudes toward it
would you say are the most biblically correct and the
most healthy?

Likewise for the family—what attitudes toward
family are the most biblically correct and the most
healthy?

9. Why is it so important to understand the negative
impact that sin has on our lives, especially in regard
to our work and family responsibilities?

10. For you, would you say your career is more of an
occupation or a preoccupation? And why?

11. Andy writes, "Because of our proclivity to veer
in the direction of things that stroke our egos,
we tend to cheat at home. We give an inordinate
amount of our time, energy, and passion to our
work." How accurately does this describe your own
situation?

12. Why are good intentions not enough when it comes to
fulfilling family responsibilities?

WEEK TWO

Chapter 3: Falling Rocks

1. In what ways can you relate to Phyllis and Jimmy's story?

2. What do you see as the most important points and principles in the "rock" parable that Andy tells here?

    How closely does this parable describe your own experiences?

Chapter 4: Picking Up the Pieces

3. Andy says that what our families want from us more than anything else is "to feel accepted. In practical terms they want to feel like they're your priority." How true would you say this is about your own family?

    How have you seen this desire demonstrated in practical ways in your family?

4. In what ways are you tempted to be more loyal to your work and career than you are to your family?

5. In this chapter Andy describes some habits used in his household to help gauge one another's emotional condition. How helpful do you think these (or something similar) could be in your family?

6. Andy emphasizes the need to "slow down long enough to check your family's vital signs." How consistently are you able to do this?

Chapter 5: Double-Edged Sword

7. As Andy continues the story of Phyllis and Jimmy in this chapter, in what ways can you relate to their experiences?

8. "To facilitate your husband's or wife's misprioritization," Andy says, "is to add to your own dysfunction." In what ways might this be happening in your own marriage and family?

    If this is a problem for you, what can you do immediately in order to change the situation?

9. As you understand it, what are the most important things to recognize about the emotional strain that results when we fail to give appropriate priority to our families?

WEEK THREE

Chapter 6: Tale of Two Kings

1. What are the most important elements in the biblical story of Daniel that are emphasized in this chapter?

2. How was Daniel's situation like your own situation?

3. How would you describe the true connection between loyalty to someone and the amount of time devoted to that person?

4. Andy notes that as we weigh what priority we'll give to work or to our families, "there's a price to pay either way you go."

    What do you see as the price you and your family will pay if you give greater priority to your work and career?

    What do you see as the likely price you'll pay in your career if you give greater priority to your family?

5. Andy speaks of the "now God" factor and the "now God" moment in Daniel's life. How does that relate to you? Has there been a "now God" factor and a "now God" moment as you've addressed the tension between work and family?

Chapter 7: Make Up Your Mind

6. What are the most important elements in Daniel's story that are emphasized in this chapter, and how do they relate to addressing the tension in your life between career and family?

7. For you, what's specifically involved in a deliberate decision to stop cheating your family?

8. Andy writes, "Following the principles of God results in the blessings of God." What benefits can you legitimately expect from making a steadfast decision to give priority to your family?

9. In what ways might there be tension in your life between family responsibilities and your involvement in sports, recreation, or hobbies?

   If this tension is there, and it raises your concern, what should you do about it?

10. Andy emphasizes the importance of asking yourself this question: "What change would your spouse most like you to make in regard to your schedule?" How would you answer that question?

11. In this chapter Andy relates much of his own experience in learning to give priority to his family. What do you appreciate most in his example?

12. In your own work, how would you analyze the relationship between productivity and actual hours spent working?

   What would you say are the most important factors influencing your productivity at work?

WEEK FOUR

Chapter 8: Create a Plan

1. What are the most important aspects of Daniel's story that are emphasized in this chapter, and how do they relate to addressing the tension in your life between career and family?

2. What are the most important elements you should include in a specific plan for giving greater priority to your family?

Chapter 9: Set Up a Test

3. What are the most important aspects of Daniel's story that are emphasized in this chapter, and how do they relate to addressing the tension in your life between career and family?

4. If you gave greater priority to your family, what effect would that have on your productivity at work? Think of a way to effectively test and measure this. What are the most important elements to include in such a trial?

5. How does your faith in God factor in to such a test?

Chapter 10: Trading Places

6. As Andy tells about Grant and Patty, in what ways can you relate their story to your own situation?

7. Andy continues the story of Joel and Marki that he began in chapter 1. How does their story relate to yours?

8. In regard to the issues discussed in this book, what does it mean for you personally to obey these words of Jesus: "Seek first His kingdom and His righteousness, and all these things will be added to you" (Matthew 6:33, NASB)?

   What can you legitimately expect God to do as a result of your obedience to these words?

9. At the end of this chapter, Andy recommends a thirty-day challenge for giving priority to your family. Are you willing to do that? If so, what will you commit to do or not do for those thirty days?

10. What things have you learned (or relearned) from going through this book that have personally helped you most?

11. What have you learned most about God and his character from this book?

12. What are you most grateful to God for as a result of going through this book?

Are you being sabotaged by your emotions?

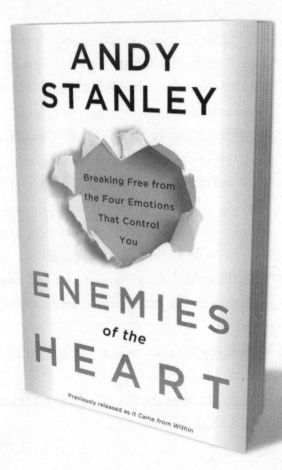

ANDY STANLEY

Breaking Free from the Four Emotions That Control You

ENEMIES of the HEART

Previously released as *It Came from Within*

Andy Stanley offers fresh biblical direction to help you overcome the destructive emotions of guilt, anger, greed, and jealousy that can control your heart.

Follow your own lead!

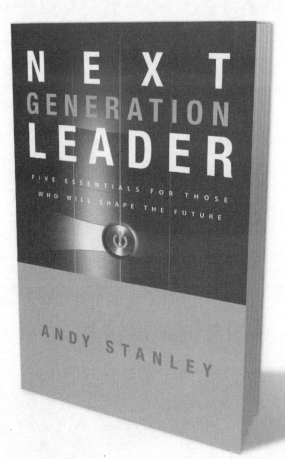

Mentoring young leaders as they face the unique issues of a changing world has been pastor and best-selling author Andy Stanley's passion for more than a decade. Here he shares material from his leadership training sessions, developed to address essential leadership qualities such as character, clarity, courage, and competency. This is the perfect guide for any new leader—or for the mentor of a future leader!

Every church leader needs to know how to win...

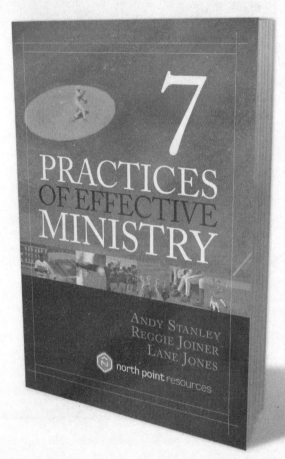

...and every congregation needs to know when to cheer. Like your own personal trainer, *7 Practices of Effective Ministry* is an insightful guide for any leader who yearns for a simpler, more effective approach to ministry. Here are seven strategic principles that when put into play will bring focus and clarity to everything you do and turn your ministry into a winning team.

When you talk, are people changed?

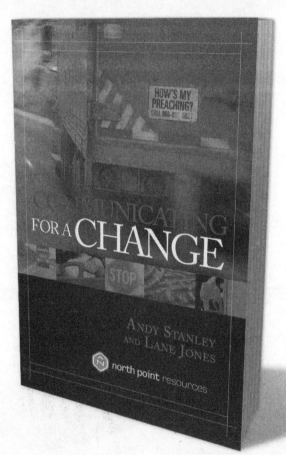

An insightful, entertaining parable that's an excellent guide for any speaker, *Communicating for a Change* takes a simple approach to speaking effectively. Join Pastor Ray as he discovers that the secrets to successful speaking are parallel to the lessons a trucker learns on the road. By knowing your destination before you leave (identifying the one basic premise of your message), using your blinkers (making transitions obvious), and implementing five other practical points, you'll drive your message home every time!

Good people go to heaven...don't they?

Surely there's more than one way to get to heaven? Bestselling author Andy Stanley addresses this popular belief held even among Christians. But believing that all good people go to heaven raises major problems, Stanley reveals. Is goodness not rewarded, then? Is Christianity not fair? Maybe not, he says. Readers will find out why Jesus taught that goodness is not even a requirement to enter heaven - and why Christianity is beyond fair. Andy Stanley leads believers and skeptics alike to a grateful awareness of God's enormous grace and mercy.